A MILLION MONKEYS

The Real Story Behind Genesis and the Meaning of Life

Dennis Patrick Treece

Copyright © 2016 Dennis Patrick Treece
All rights reserved.

ISBN: 1537797654
ISBN 13: 9781537797656
Library of Congress Control Number: 2016915888
CreateSpace Independent Publishing Platform
North Charleston, South Carolina

PREFACE

"A million monkeys typing will, given sufficient time, write something known, like Hamlet."

One of many possible variations of the million monkey theorem by Émile Borel

This narrative contains a simple message: there is a God, our Creator. He has provided the Universe with some simple rules, and He is expecting them to be followed eventually in a conscious, competent manner, as evidenced by the choices we make. Unfortunately, humanity is failing to do what is expected of it—which is a problem for us and by extension the rest of all Creation. Just because of human behavior. You might well ask how we got into this mess. The answer seems simple until you start looking at it more closely.

Like everything else that evolved as the Universe expanded, we humans weren't inevitable, only possible. Think about it. We developed into what we are today through countless random chemical and biological events, but there was no guarantee we would ever exist at all, much less in the way we are now. But after some billions of our years, we find ourselves where we are today, one outcome out of who knows how many possible outcomes. It's like the million monkeys typing. Given enough time, all possible outcomes will eventually be realized no matter how unlikely they might seem.

But here's the thing: humanity is and has been for a long time, at a tipping point. The crisis is based on the sad facts that human behavior is essentially negative, has a negative ripple effect upon all of Creation, and shows no sign of improving. Our predilection toward negativity and violence in all their forms means we are more likely than not to row our boat in the opposite direction from the rest of Creation. Fixing this is simple for us to say but hard for us to do. Think more Loving thoughts. Say more Loving words. Do more Loving things. Don't sweat the small stuff. Relax. Don't default to Hate; rather, default to Love.

Of course, the devil is in the details. Keep reading to learn what they are.

TABLE OF CONTENTS

Section One Narrator's Introduction	1
1 How This Began for Me	3
2 Introduction to the Narrative	8
Section Two The Universe	11
3 Vibrational Existence	13
• Vibrational Planes	13
• The Physical Planes	14
• The Earth Plane	18
4 Thought Creation	22
• Thought Energy	22
• Thought Creation	23
• The Power of Prayer	26
Section Three The Creator, Creation, and the Divine Plan	29
5 The Divine One	31
6 Genesis	34
7 Reunification is the Divine Plan	37

Section Four	What You Are and Who You Are	41
8	Souls	43
9	Human Beings	48
10	The Human-Soul Partnership	53
11	The Divine in Each of You	59
Section Five	The Meaning of Life	61
12	The Meaning of Life	63
13	Clarifying and Reinforcing the Process of Learning	68
14	The Conditions Under Which You Learn Are Essential	71
	• How The Universe Works	71
	• The Sanctity of Life	74
	• Good and Evil, Love and Hate	75
	• Pain and Suffering	80
	• Divine Intervention	85
Section Six	What Happens When You "Die"	93
15	Heaven and Hell	95
16	Judgment	101
	• Reflection and Remorse	101
	• Judgment	104
	• Consequences	107
	• Punishment	108
17	What Comes Next	111
About the Author		113

Section Seven	Epilogue, Glossary	115
Epilogue		117
Glossary		123

SECTION ONE

Narrator's Introduction

1

HOW THIS BEGAN FOR ME

"Sometimes I believe in as many as six impossible things before breakfast."

Alice, *from* **Alice in Wonderland**, *by* **Lewis Carroll**

In an airplane climbing out of a cloudy, chilly London morning into a bright autumn sky in 2008, I was on my way back to the States and wondering how I would pass the six or so hours of the flight. Then I heard a voice in my head: "Get a pen and paper; you are going to write." For nearly the entire flight, I listened and wrote the messages that came into my mind from wherever. I asked questions, I got answers, and I wrote it all down. I've been processing these messages ever since. I've also been asking more questions and getting more answers. I was not the one who chose the title of this narrative. You will see its relevance as you read on.

Why me? Why am I the one writing this? I have no idea, really. I think I'm an unlikely candidate. I'm a non-religious combat-wounded army veteran who has spent thirty years going about the business of protecting my country and its interests in the world. After my military service, I worked in computer network security for a couple of years and ran an airport and seaport security program for eleven years before deciding to fully retire. These experiences do not give me any credentials to write what you will read here. I am just the unlikely messenger, narrating the story as best I can with no vested interest in whether you believe any of it or not. That said, I have taken my role as narrator seriously and have worked hard to accurately and faithfully present what was given to me.

I want to be crystal clear about this: the information and message presented in this narrative do not come from me. The Spirit Guide who is providing me this information identifies as a Super-Soul of some magnitude but does not give me any name. (For information on souls, see the glossary and chapter 8.) The Super-Soul is telling me it's an "Earth specialist" because most of the physical incarnations by all of its merged souls have been on Earth. It tells me these many tens of thousands of lives have experienced every form of human behavior, both good and evil, before attaining Enlightenment and then Perfection.

Even though I am faithful in conveying the information I've been given, this Guide tells me there is much more that I don't know and am not supposed to know, and apparently neither are you. I can pass along to you only what I have been given. The message I am delivering at the insistence of this Guide is simple, and I have been given some supporting material to make the final message more clear and compelling. That's really all there is to it.

My understanding of the concepts and information put into my head is sometimes cloudy, especially when I don't have the words to process them. I can't explain the process other than to say the information is suddenly in my head. It usually doesn't come as a narrative, but rather all at once, like a memory. It's like remembering something. I just have it in my mind all of a sudden. What helps me believe this is really happening is that sometimes when I ask a question about a message, I get an answer in the same way. But the message is often difficult to put into words because it does not usually come in words. There are a few direct quotes in this narrative, however, and I am grateful for them since they require no search for the right words. Another helpful aspect to my writing is what I call "guided typing." Through automatic writing, people have written in longhand what some Spirit is telling them. This has not happened with me, but many times while I'm typing, I can "feel" the presence of the Guide, which is definitely helping me translate its thoughts into words. Here is an example of the difficulty: let's say I am shown in my head a fourth primary color. How do I describe it for you? There is no frame of reference we share for this new color. I can see it in my mind, but I can't explain it. There is no name for it, here on Earth, and in fact our vibration doesn't support it, which is why we don't have it. And so it is with some aspects of the Universe that simply don't (and can't) manifest here. When I have trouble with certain subjects, I do get some help, but it can be fuzzy. It seems these topics are right on the boundary of what we need to know versus what we are allowed to know. I am advised that too much information would make it easier for us to "guess" our way through our individual spiritual journeys. That would be close to cheating. Instead, we have to "work" our way forward.

Another point to make is that there is, or ought to be, a vast majesty to the revelations here. These are answers to the basic questions of humankind ever since human thought has had the luxury to stray from where to find the next meal. I apologize for not being able to put the proper drama into the words I present. It's easy to see why organized religions build lofty cathedrals and temples and mosques with magnificent architecture and have music, fine clothing, and wonderful rituals. These are designed to move people in spiritual ways. It is also easy to understand why many holy books are adorned with illuminations and beautiful bindings. Without it, the majesty of a message can be lost in its simplicity and unadorned brevity. Having said that, I am certain that my plain presentation here may be some of the most important kilobytes you will ever read.

Some, maybe even most of the information here, is not new. I make no claim that I am unique in any way or that I have a special relationship with The Divine. These topics have been delivered to us humans and written about and speculated upon throughout history. A wealth of information is published all the time about spiritual and religious topics. The many examples in films and print media show how many people have written about these same concepts, though using different words. The Divine One's special messengers, like my Guide, have likely always shared information about who we are, what we are, and why we are here. This is, I suppose, why many religions and religious philosophies contain common elements on these themes.

While this narrative is not filled with complete happiness, I am hopeful that many of you will find your own peace with it. The intent is to help all the voices out there reinforcing love and understanding, peace, and compassion, for a human race that sorely needs more of these things.

2

INTRODUCTION TO THE NARRATIVE

"If we do discover a complete theory, it should in time be understandable in broad principle by everyone, not just a few scientists. Then we shall all, philosophers, scientists, and just ordinary people, be able to take part in the discussion of the question of why it is that we and the universe exist. If we find the answer to that, it would be the ultimate triumph of human reason— for then we would know the mind of God."

Stephen Hawking

Well, Stephen, hang on to your hat. What follows in these pages is the actual story of our Universe, The Creator, humankind's relationship with Him, and the Meaning of Life, among other fundamentals of our existence.

I once heard someone say, "Faith is our answer for the incomprehensible." We take certain answers to questions about the nature of God and the meaning of life on faith because there is no alternative. There is simply no way to prove these things in any practical or scientific way. If we feel comfortable with what we call "matters of faith," then we make them part of our belief systems. We defend them in spite of the fact that they are unprovable and indefensible. They are simply what we believe. It is for this reason that Spirit has not provided all the answers for me to pass on to you in this narrative. Otherwise, there would be no room left for faith, and faith is a necessary component to our progress here.

To most readers, this narrative will be beyond belief. But whether you believe it or not, *it is what it is.* I would not characterize the message here as happy. While we all naturally want to hear nothing but good things about ourselves, our situations, and our futures, that's not what comes through here. Rather, I should characterize this narrative as essentially a reality check and wake-up call. It will inevitably rattle some established religions, but that's understandable. All human institutions eventually overreach, and this takes them away from their original good intentions.

At its core, this narrative clarifies where humankind is in relation to the Divine One, and the Universe He created, in order that we may receive and heed the underlying message. The underlying message that will be laid out here is that we are too prone to hate things and events not to our liking and people we find inconvenient, difficult, in our way, prettier, richer, smarter, and more successful than we are. In short, we sweat the small stuff and often make it big stuff.

Please note that the information from Section Two through the Epilogue and Glossary of Terms is from my Guide and is written in its voice and addressed to all of humanity. In the few instances where I feel it necessary to provide a personal comment or anecdote to clarify something, *I have noted it is from me, the narrator, and have put it in italics.* Information of particular importance is also in italics but it is not from me unless it clearly says "Narrator". All of the quotations are identified by each author, whom my Guide led me to on the Internet. The quotations show how the subject matter presented here has been addressed elsewhere for a great many years by a great many people.

So ready or not, what you will read here is information about the ultimately Original Thing, or Origin of Everything and how it is intended to play out—what it means to us on what is known as The Earth Plane and indeed, what it all means to God, who henceforth will almost always be referred to as the Divine One.

SECTION TWO

The Universe

3

VIBRATIONAL EXISTENCE

"If you want to find the secrets of the universe, think in terms of energy, frequency, and vibration."

Nikola Tesla

Vibrational Planes

The common denominator throughout the Universe is that everything has a specific vibrational rate, or frequency, that helps define it. These vibrations are what "assign" things to their levels of existence. The Universe holds a vast number of vibrational levels and types of existence, most of which are nonphysical. Perhaps the first thing to understand is that there is so much more to the Universe than what you can see or feel or hear or taste or smell on Earth. Most of the Universe is, in fact, energetic and not physical at all. No discussion of the whole Universe can be complete without acknowledging that the majority of it is simply beyond your perception. Human language and science are not advanced enough to provide the proper terms to correctly explain this further. You can't just Google your way to a clearer understanding on this.

So everything, including People, are harmonic. Everything. All of it. The whole kit and caboodle. The Divine One, the big bang, the Universe, right on down to the smallest of all identifiable particles or energies, are vibrations, whether physical or not.

The Physical Planes
Of course, the Universe has a physical aspect. You know this because you live in it, and you can experience at least this much by using your five senses. The physical plane is at the bottom—the slowest level—of all the vibrational spectra in the Universe. The Physical Plane has many vibrational levels, and Earth is on one of them. A large global community of people accepts as much about the Universe, but this narrative is not meant just for them. The reason it is being provided now is to fill a need for humans of every faith and persuasion to understand the fundamental concept of vibrational planes and their separation, how this is manifest throughout the Universe, and what it means to them. Without that awareness, no explanation of The Divine One and the Universe or your role in it is likely to produce any understanding whatsoever.

Narrator: Most of you are not scientists, and neither am I. But let me tell you how I first became aware of the concept of vibrational differences, which I now know define the various energy planes. This anecdote may help you, as it helped me, understand this basic concept. Many years ago, while walking in the woods in North Carolina, I happened on a big old tree with an eighteen-inch strand of rusty barbed wire sticking out of it about four feet off the ground. I was curious about this sight, and then I noticed that another piece of rusty barbed wire was sticking out of the tree, at a ninety-degree angle to the first one, at the same distance off the ground. At first, I thought it odd that somebody would drill holes into a tree and stick rusty barbed wire into them. Then it hit me that this had been a corner post of a fenced-in field at some time when the tree was much younger and much thinner. Over time, the tree grew around the wire until it appeared to be coming from the middle of the tree. Apparently, the fence was removed at some point and the landowner, for whatever reason, left these two pieces of wire sticking out of the tree. These pieces of wire got me to thinking—and this is where my guided "intuition" came in—not about the farmer or the field, but about the tree and the humans who have come and gone throughout its life. It seemed that the tree lived at a much slower pace than people. Does the tree even notice us? Would we look, to the tree, like a bit of film moving impossibly fast? Or would we move so fast as to be invisible to the tree? If that was the case, could it be that other people around me were moving so fast that I could not see them or hear them or feel them? And, likewise, that they would not hear me or see me or feel me? How many worlds can coexist in such a fashion? Well, how many entertainment channels can travel down the same fiber-optic cable? Same idea. We read fictional stories about alternate worlds and universes, and perhaps this is the way they coexist. Standing there, I smiled and thought that this was a bit much to get out of barbed wire sticking out of a tree. But then where do new ideas and perceptions come from if not fragments of other ideas, other voices, other rooms, or, indeed, The Divine (by way of our Spirit Guides)? My thinking did not stop there. Perhaps this was even the explanation for UFOs and space aliens. Perhaps they don't travel the vastness of space to get here; they are already "here." What they have learned how to do is change their rate of vibration so they can move from one physical vibration

> *and world to another without going between stars in outer space. And the reason they are normally off the ground (in a spaceship) when spotted is that they do not want to materialize in our vibration inside a building or mountain, so they have to get high enough to miss even the tallest mountains. Crazy? Does not seem so to me, especially now.*

On the physical plane, you are at the lowest vibrational rate in Creation, as is everything you are able to observe and measure. You are not able to directly observe or measure anything outside (above or next to) your own vibration no matter how you might speculate the existence of such things. Some of us "up here" refer to your Plane as the mud level. Compared with the rest of Existence, you move slowly, constricted by your slow vibrational rate. It's sort of like being mired in a big glob of thick mud. Everything physical, humans included, are in a sense "trapped" at, and within, their native vibrational band, the one they were born into.

That said, a vibration faster than but just one level above the Earth's physical vibration is where souls go first when liberated from their human hosts—upon the death of the host. That vibration is outside your present field of view but close enough to be visible and audible, under the right conditions, and more by some people than by others. Mediums can do this. When a soul at that higher level of vibration wants to get a message to you on your side of the divide, it tries to do so through a medium if one is near you. Otherwise, the soul may try the direct approach, which entails lowering its vibration while trying to coax you to raise your own vibration, whether you are aware of it or not. Most often, this does not work because most humans are not sensitive to this capability. Attempts at contact between the planes sometimes can explain light-bulb explosions and audio equipment interference. It also explains some ghostly images in photographs that nobody seems to understand. Electronic devices are especially susceptible to the vibrational activity that results when these two Planes of Existence interact.

The vibrations above Earth increase in stages until they reach the highest, most rapid level, where The Divine One resides. Larger, more powerful merged souls can move down, or "visit" lower vibrations than themselves, but not up. The only way to move up is to "graduate" up. Without the "drag" of the Physical Plane, more things can and do happen at higher vibrational levels. One thing that can happen is thought creation, a concept that is essential to understanding the Universe at large. Thought creation will be discussed in the next chapter.

The Earth Plane
There are more souls than there are humans to host them, so we are all fortunate to have alternatives to human form on the Earth Plane. Animals, plants,

mountains, rivers, and all manner of other things will support energetic partnerships. People from many cultures have long believed that there is consciousness in the rocks and trees around them. And so there is. The most common path for incarnation on the Earth plane is progression upward from the inanimate to the animate, and ultimately to a human partner.

You are on the Earth Plane right now because you (your soul) has made the choice to be there. Thinking of it as a school or an arena would not be far off the mark. From The Divine One's perspective, the Physical Plane experience, Earth included, is a form of intense testing of souls, and the human being is the most effective, efficient "training aid" in all of Creation. That is not by design, but simply the way it has worked out. This testing is designed to identify the soul's progress along the path of Enlightenment toward Perfection. This identification, or assessment, is achieved through observation of your behavior throughout a lifetime of challenging situations. So no matter how difficult your life is on Earth, you are privileged to be there. You have been given the opportunity to Learn in ways you can't manage as just an energy being. On the Earth plane, your parents might starve you to death. A building might fall on you. A stranger might shoot you in a dark alley for the change in your pockets. You can die in a plane or car crash. At no other level of existence will a witless driver slaughter your family while texting on a cell phone. Stuff happens on Earth. There is much to be Learned from these situations, both as saint and sinner, victim and perpetrator. There is equally as much to be Learned from loving parents, good health, financial well-being, friendships, children, the sweet smell of a freshly mowed lawn, the feeling of a cool breeze on a hot day, the taste of delicious food, finding your soul mate, and winning the lottery. All of life's experiences, both good and bad, help you Learn because they all offer you choices to make. It is in those choices, and the actions that follow, where you demonstrate either success in moving forward, or being "stuck" in bad choices, or even falling behind. Some people recognize where they are in this journey to Learn better behavior while still on the Earth Plane. For many, if not most, however, this understanding happens only after the physical body dies and the soul is in its post-physical life review.

When you went to your Earth experience, you put your knowledge of the Divine behind you, to be recovered upon your physical death, so you might fully experience and benefit from the wonders of a sensuous, irrational, conflict-driven, physical life. You are on the level of existence where you sit in The Divine One's Schoolhouse for the privilege of Learning, and it is one tough place. For much of human development, the choices have been to kill or be killed, eat or be eaten, and breed or face extinction. The level of violence there has not really diminished over time. You are perpetually at war with each other as nations, religions, tribes, and families. Although humans know how to behave nicely and understand the value of the Golden Rule, too many ignore their kinder instincts on a regular basis. So it is on Earth where you have such wonderful opportunities to Learn fundamental lessons that help the soul realize The Divine One's Plan by Learning to behave properly—if you can only manage to do so.

4

THOUGHT CREATION

"Believe something and the Universe is on its way to being changed. Because you've changed, by believing. Once you've changed, other things start to follow. Isn't that the way it works?"

Diane Duane

Thought Energy

"Thoughts are energy and represent the energy force of the universe."

Rev. Dr. Eleanor Ruth Fisher

Before any discussion of thought creation, it is important to understand thoughts and thought energy. Every human and every soul and every other conscious part of the Divine has thoughts. These thoughts consist of two aspects: the thought energy behind them and their content. This is kind of like the Internet. An Internet service provider gives access to the Internet but does not provide content. Conscious energies like you do that. And so it is with thoughts. In essence, the Divine One has provided all conscious energies with access to The Universe through their thoughts, and all these conscious energies are responsible for what those thoughts contain. There are no limits to their content. Given that all conscious energies have Free Will and given that their thoughts are not controlled, thoughts cover the entire spectrum of all possible subject matter and emotions. Some are kind and gentle, and some are hateful and hurtful. The important thing to know is that all thoughts in the Universe are palpable. They are also available throughout the Universe, and the Divine One and His assistants hear them and "feel" them, both as they happen and forever. Human thoughts are especially powerful. This was not by design but simply because of the way humans have developed. As a result of their unusual power and high vibration, human thoughts can be "felt" from one end of the Universe to the other. More on that later.

Thought Creation

Thought creation is a consequence of thought energy. It was, for example, The Divine One's "thought" that created the Universe we know today and all of the processes within it. Only the Divine One has the power to make something like that happen with a thought, but all conscious energies (souls) at every magnitude possess sufficient power for thought creation. The more power available to any soul or collection of souls, the more options for thought creation are available. While thought creation is a given throughout most of the Universe, it is mostly not possible at the slow vibrational rate of the physical planes, including the Earth Plane. The energetic "mud" of physical existence simply resists thought creation unless there is sufficient thought energy to overcome that resistance. Thought creation escapes understanding by the majority of the Earthbound because it generally makes no sense on that plane. On the higher-vibration planes, called the Energy Planes or Spirit Planes, thought creation is a given. All a Spirit needs to do to have something or be somewhere or be doing something is to think of it. If they think of standing on the north rim of the Grand Canyon at sunset, there they are. If they think they are in the center of a star, there they are. If they think they are enjoying a caramel latte while sitting in their favorite chair and listening to their favorite music with Spirits they are attached to, there they are just as they "thought" it.

> *Narrator: There is a wonderful 1998 Universal Studios movie with Robin Williams called* What Dreams May Come. *The*

> *story line is not important here, but when Robin Williams's character dies, he is in a place where thoughts dictate the setting, including the weather, the plants, a beloved pet who has died, etc. This is an accurate visual depiction of a thought-created universe. You merely have to think it, and there it all is.*

The reason you need to know about thought creation and the power of thoughts is that they are tangible and for all intents and purposes "physical" manifestations that are loosed on the Universe. The inherent power behind human thoughts is also why people who do not believe in the power of prayer can negate their own prayers and even the prayers of others for them with their own "anti-prayer" thoughts. If you think prayer is foolish, ineffective, or a waste of time, then for you they are. The thing to remember is that thoughts are powerful, tangible above the physical planes, and not perishable. This is why hate, anger, jealousy, and so forth, are unwelcome throughout Creation. What most people don't realize is how harmful these negative thoughts are outside their own lives. All thoughts, good and bad, are forever- kind of like putting something on the Internet. They reverberate throughout the Cosmos and are forever identified with their originators. As a result, the Universe is under a kind of constant surveillance by the Divine One and His assistants, whether or not you know it or like it. It is as if the Creator has a recording device with infinite storage capacity that is wired to every speck of substance (including thoughts) in Creation. All of it is noted when it happens, but it is also available for review whenever appropriate—such as after you die and review the substance of your life and how you have affected the lives of other people and other things. This is how you are held accountable and judged for what you do—both the good things and the bad things.

The Power of Prayer

> *"All I know is that when I pray, coincidences happen; and when I don't pray, they don't happen."*
>
> *Dan Hayes*

Prayer is a form of focused, purposeful thought. It is a form of intention. Prayer is your human way of calling on Divine help in all of its forms. Prayer enables you to tap into the powers available on the energy planes in order to perform acts of healing, mediumship, past life readings, etc. To work, though, prayer must be sincere. Prayer performed for show without honest intent behind it is not prayer and does not work.

What is the power of prayer? Call it Divine Energy if that makes more sense to you. It permeates everything in the Universe, keeps everything in constant "awareness" of everything else, and carries vast amounts of information, energy, and power. You can and do make use of this Force, and one of the best ways is through prayer. Groups of people and their souls can join in thoughts and prayers to add their strength to the thoughts and intentions expressed. This is a temporary way to boost the prayer's power and is helpful in obtaining the desired result. If sufficient Divine power is applied to any matter at hand, you can achieve thought creation on your plane. The result can be described as a miracle. And so it is. This is one of the exceptions to the lack of thought creation on the physical plane. With sufficient thought energy and the right intention, it can be done.

There are limitations on your use of this power of prayer for obvious reasons. If you were meant to tap into these resources as a matter of course for your everyday life on Earth, there would be little or no purpose for souls to be there at all.

SECTION THREE

The Creator, Creation, and the Divine Plan

5

THE DIVINE ONE

"You can never solve a problem on the same level of thinking in which it was created."

Albert Einstein

If you believe in any supreme being, then you will have formed some notion of what that belief means to you. Perhaps you simply rely on clergy from your chosen faith to tell you all about your Divine Being. In truth, none of you can fully understand The Divine One's nature. Einstein was exactly right when he noted that no question can be answered without a relevant frame of reference. You there in human forms on the Physical Plane simply lack any way to adequately understand the nature of a Divine Force so far outside your own experience or imaginations. As this narrative unfolds, you will form your own opinions about who you are and how this all came about, and that's fine and as it should be. The people who take this narrative as written will simply be ahead of everyone else in understanding what their lives are really about.

The message to humanity being delivered here must begin with an exploration of the true nature of The Divine One, because all life, in fact all of everything, springs from this Source.

The Divine One is not a man-like thing or a woman-like thing. This is a being of pure energy (which encompasses all matter) that makes up the sum total of everything that is now and ever was and ever will be, including you—both body and soul. The Divine One is an intelligent and powerful presence so vast and all-encompassing that you may only guess at it. Even then, the guess will fall way short of the truth. This is why your "accepted" religious texts of all sorts reduce the Divine One to measurable, understandable, comfortable, man-like (if grand) characters. The reality is just too overwhelming to comprehend.

Even so, the question remains, "Who or what is the Divine One? The answer is that the Divine One is everything, everywhere, and every when. There is nothing that is not the Divine One. Period. The Divine One is timeless, present, and aware of every form of "being," both physical and pure energy. He exists simultaneously in the past, in the present, and in the future. He experiences everything that has ever happened, is happening, and will happen. This is at the atomic and subatomic levels across the whole of Creation, and is both physical and nonphysical. The Divine One experiences every cell that divides, every movement of every sun that burns, every atom of every frozen asteroid in the deepest, coldest parts of space, every human smile that has ever formed, and every human tear that has ever been shed. Every emotion, every thought, every deed, and every consequence both real and imagined are known to The Divine One, and have been and are being experienced by the Divine One. Everything.

It is also important to know that the Divine One is Love, pure Love, and Love is the Divine One, and the Divine One is total. The Divine One is *everything*—now and for always. And everything is Love, and Love is everything.

Everything that makes you what you are and how you are constructed is the Divine One because the Divine One is everything. Every emotion you feel is felt by the Divine One. Everything you do is experienced by the Divine One. Everything you know is known by the Divine One. There is nothing you can ever do, see, feel, taste, smell, or hear that is not at the same time done, seen, felt, tasted, smelled, or heard by the Divine One. All of that is also remembered by the Divine One. If you can be bored, so can the Divine One. If you can feel joy, so can the Divine One. And so He does. Just remember that your physical body is made up of the Divine One's essence and your soul is a conscious, energetic sliver of the Divine One Himself.

6

GENESIS

"Whenever the rainbow appears in the clouds I shall see it and remember the everlasting covenant between God and all living creatures on the earth."

Genesis 9:16

Why are things the way they are? Because that's the way the Divine One designed them to be way back at the beginning. That is, *the Beginning of Everything*.

This next part might take some getting used to. But keep an open mind, and remember that it does not matter if you believe it or not right now, only that you know the story. It will percolate in your sub consciousness until you are ready to deal with it and perhaps eventually embrace it.

"In the beginning…" there was just the Divine One. There was nothing else—any "where" or any "when."

And it was not good because it was not interesting and not productive. Imagine being the Divine One, capable of being and creating anything either physical or energetic, and not doing so. Well, it was the Divine One's determination—his "thought," if you will—that created everything.

And so it was that with due deliberation and incredible insight and foresight, and in an instant, yes <u>that</u> "instant", the Big Bang was the Divine One setting everything into motion by simply thinking it into action.

BANG!

In an instant, the Divine One went from being a single whole entity into millions of billions of trillions of fragments of Himself. The Old Testament's Book of Genesis refers to this closely. "In the beginning the Earth was without form and void and darkness was on the face of the deep. And God said, 'Let there be light!' And there was light.". Etc. The people who wrote that were getting the same message provided to you here and now. They just wrote it in their language or passed it orally from generation to generation, and it has been translated or edited many times in many languages ever since. A more accurate version would go like this: "In the beginning there was only the Divine One and nothing else, and darkness was on the face of the Divine, and the Divine One said, 'Out of Myself, Let there be Action!'" And instead of "Let there be Light," the Divine One essentially said, "Let there be Chaos." Yes, He had, and still has, a Divine Plan, what some people might refer to as "Intelligent Design" but refers to much more than the creation of humankind.

In the instant of Creation all that is, was, and shall be fragmented into what you know of as The Universe. The Divine One was exactly all of it, and yet now more than before. The reason the whole is now greater than the sum of its parts is that now there is *activity*, and with that activity the Divine One was and is increased by the experiences taking place in an interactive universe now suddenly in both random and intelligent *motion*. Before the Big Bang, the Divine One was everything, as in *everything*. After the Big Bang, the Divine One was still everything but there were now a vast number of individual, moving, sometimes thinking, parts of the former single entity. These things, these independent moving parts of the Divine, throughout all of creation, were and are doing all manner of activities—randomly, chaotically, and consciously—instead of just being a single infinitely aware Totality. Why did the Divine One do it? ***Because it is far more meaningful for even the Divine One to have a purpose for existence than to simply exist.***

7

REUNIFICATION IS THE DIVINE PLAN

"All the king's horses and all the king's men couldn't put Humpty Dumpty together again."

James William Elliott

As amazing as the creation story is, the thing to focus on is what happened after the Big Bang put everything into motion. You need to be aware of it so you can embrace your Divine heritage and responsibility. What follows is an explanation of the Divine One's purpose for Creation.

All of Creation following the creation event is Divine substance, but not all of this substance is conscious. The conscious substance in the Universe is all fragments of the Divine and what you commonly think of as souls. Everyone has one, and there are many more souls than you can comprehend. All of these souls are scattered throughout Creation, coexisting with the unconscious fragments of the Divine. These Divine conscious fragments, or souls, are the entities that the Divine One has charged with fulfilling His Plan. These are the decision-makers. Like humans, they can decide to do good things or they can decide to do not-so-good (wrong) things. The more inexperienced they are, the more prone they are to doing the wrong things.

While the Divine One retains His identity and cohesive thoughts, He is "fragmented" into a multitude of pieces scattered throughout Creation. He is enjoying the interplay among all those fragments, but His goal is for them to coalesce, eventually, back into a single whole: ***Him.*** He established a process for this Divine Reunification based on some simple actions. This is a process whereby the pieces join together, one by one, once certain conditions have been met, until they are all back together again.

The conditions for Reunification—that is, the underlying rules of the game plan— involve all souls and may be summarized as follows:

1. It is essential to the Plan that all souls have Free Will. This allowed for the independence of action that could lead to both good and bad choices. These choices, these decisions, result in independent and random action throughout Creation.

2. It is essential that all souls be ignorant of the Plan at the beginning of their individual journeys. Not knowing the purpose for their journeys enables souls to figure it out for themselves by experiencing all ranges of activity, both good and bad, and by demonstrating, eventually, that they "get it" and stop making the wrong choices and doing bad things.
3. It is essential that the Divine One not be an active participant in this process. If the Divine One were actively involved, the playing field would not be level and results would not be completely random, which would invalidate His Plan.

The independence given these souls is what you know as Free Will, which is the only law the souls must follow. This independence of action sets up the condition that needs to be met that will enable the Divine One to be put back together again. And the condition for Reunification is for all souls to *reject Hate in favor of Love, as evidenced by the choices they make in their thoughts, words, and deeds.*

Have you ever watched how liquid mercury behaves? It can be taken from a cohesive drop of liquid metal and separated into such minute particles that they resemble paint. But when these particles touch one another under certain circumstances, they merge into larger droplets and continue to join one another until they are back into a single drop of liquid metal. So it is with souls, or "droplets," of the Divine One.

The end state of all this merging is that the Divine One is Whole again. This means that, if everything goes as planned, we will all someday be reunited into the whole of God, which is Everything, which is pure Love. And this is where the million monkey theorem applies. Under the theorem, there should be every reason to believe that all possible outcomes, including Reunification, will happen, given sufficient time. This is true no matter how likely or unlikely the possible outcomes are. So under the conditions that have been set for all souls to achieve Reunification, no matter how difficult or unlikely, it should eventually happen, if the theorem is correct. The assumption must be that the million monkeys will bang away at their typewriters in a random, incoherent manner. So as long as souls behave randomly in their Spiritual Journeys while still in the ignorant "monkey" stage of their progress, they should all Learn enough to see the bigger picture. They may begin to work consciously on furthering the Divine Plan. At that point, they are no longer "monkeys" and do not interfere with the theorem. *With the Universe as the vehicle, the Divine One is essentially challenging this theorem and using His own "life" to do it.*

It is, therefore, our Divine right and our Divine responsibility, both humans and souls of all magnitudes, to work to achieve this Reunification. In this, all conscious parts of Creation may be thought of as "all the King's Horses and all the King's Men" working to put Humpty Dumpty together again.

SECTION FOUR

What You Are and Who You Are

8

SOULS

"For truly we are all angels temporarily hiding as humans."

Brian L. Weiss

People are often heard to remark, "He or she is an old soul." What they usually mean is that the person has a mature, kind, and gentle way of behaving. This is a nice sentiment to apply to anyone, but the truth is that all souls are exactly the same age. Regardless of where each soul is on its spiritual path, all of us are parts of the same Divine Source, ageless and immortal.

While you are reading this through human eyes and with a human brain, "You" are at once human and spirit. The Spirit part of you, your soul, is an immortal energy being that has partnered with your human body since before birth. As a result, there has been a mutually beneficial partnership that ends when the human dies. Then your soul moves on. Those who wish to see the human and the soul as a single entity have simply got it wrong. They must be separate because one dies and the other does not.

The terms "soul" and "spirit" in this narrative mean the same thing. It is not to say, however, that all souls or spirits are equal. They once were, back at the Beginning, but some souls have achieved more Enlightenment and Perfection than others and have merged with other Enlightened and Perfected souls to create Compound-Souls and Super-Souls. Compound-Souls are well on their way to Perfection, having achieved Enlightenment, and have merged with other Enlightened souls. Super-Souls have achieved Perfection and have merged with other Perfect souls but have not yet merged with the Divine One Himself. What changes as all souls merge is the magnitude of their Essence. The greater the number of Enlightened souls in a "pod" of Compound-Souls, the greater understanding it will have, the greater power it will have, the greater responsibility and authority it will have. The same is true for Super-Souls, which form from the merger of pods of Compound-Souls that have achieved Perfection. The more Perfected souls there are in a "pod" of Super-Souls, the greater understanding, power, responsibility, and authority it will have.

Compound-Souls and Super-Souls are still simply agents of the Divine One, like the simple-souls most humans have, but they have much more Divine Energy along with increased authority and responsibility. All merged souls at whatever magnitude combine the memories of all the things they had to endure and all the lessons they had to Learn in order to achieve Enlightenment and then Perfection. Their identities are therefore complex and helpful as they pursue the accomplishment of the Divine Plan. These advanced souls of all magnitudes manifest on Earth physically and energetically as saintly people and angels. Because you have a soul, you need to stop thinking of yourself as just human. Rather, you need to think of yourself as both human and Spirit. This is a complex partnership that is not easy to understand, although an attempt is made here to help you do that.

A lot of souls specialize in various aspects of the workings of the Universe, but only the Divine One knows everything and has the ability to be, know, and do everything.

On the energy planes, all souls have the ability to be anywhere and any when, consistent with their levels of vibration. In your Spirit form, you may remain on the spiritual planes or visit the physical plane. Humans who can, through training and meditation, connect with their souls directly are able to do what is commonly known as "astral traveling" and experience what it is like to go anywhere with the power of thought.

When in Spirit form, free of your physical life, you are able to observe the lives of your physically living family and friends. You may also try to assist them through the help of a Medium or even directly. You can also partner your soul-energy with non-human and even non-living things on the physical plane to achieve more focused experiences. This is helpful in your individual journey as a soul because it helps you understand the complex experiences, trials, and temptations of all physical beings. Those that do this have choices to partner with things such as any sort of animal, insect, or plant, and even "nonliving" things such as rocks, mountains, lakes, or rivers.

When a soul is first selected to experience the Earth plane, it will not start out as a partner to a human being. It is more likely to be partnered with a so-called lower life form or even an inanimate object to experience life on this planet or another planet on a physical plane. Let's say you go in for the first time as lichen growing on a boulder high on some mountain on Earth. You will experience the sun, the wind, the rain, the snow, the seasons, storms, and the inexorable growth of your lichen body and the slow deterioration of the rock that is your host. Your choices will be limited, and therefore your ability to Learn will be restricted in the extreme. Depending on what your Guides have in mind, you eventually can move up to more active sojourns on Earth as a bug or a dog or a cat or a rabbit or an eagle. Ultimately, you may be given the opportunity to experience life with an apex host, a human being. Along the way on these journeys, you will experience what it is to eat and be eaten by a fellow creature. You run away as best you can to avoid being eaten. If you are the predator, then you chase as well as you can in order to eat. Of course, everything living on Earth must eat to survive. Big fish eat smaller fish and in turn are eaten by bigger fish. No malice in that, just survival. The malice will come when you are allowed to partner with the "higher" life form, the apex predator, a human. This is so important because, unlike most other life forms on Earth, humans are routinely lured toward the "dark side" of all emotions. Therein lies the reason your soul is partnered with your human host in the first place.

9

HUMAN BEINGS

"On the whole, we're a murderous race. According to Genesis, it took as few as four people to make the planet too crowded to stand, and the first murder was a fratricide."

Jim Butcher

Many people want to think that humans were created by God in His image. Well, it is not so because "God" isn't a physical being and has no "image" as you know it. The Divine One's essence is what makes up everything, both energetic and physical, so an argument might be made that you are of, by, and for the Divine so must be in His image. But once again, it just isn't so. You are of His Essence, not His Image.

Remember, humans weren't inevitable—only possible. The random acts of chemistry and biology that resulted in the human being were special throughout all of Creation. Humans are the most challenging beings anywhere—not because that is the way it is supposed to be, but simply the way things have turned out. Kill or be killed. Eat or be eaten. Breed or face extinction. That has been the environment on the dangerous physical planet Earth for all species, not just humans. To survive and thrive, humans developed as violence-prone adversity-conquering specialists with great intelligence and powerful thoughts. It is interesting, however, that human development has been affected by the constant presence of soul partners. In fact, the whole notion of natural selection is skewed in some ways by the continuous presence of the energy being called the soul. This has not worked out in a negative way. In fact, it has been a distinct advantage. More in the beginning of your development than at present, the soul partner has assisted humanity to survive against all odds, given that it takes so long to raise humans to be viable enough to protect themselves against other animals and other humans.

In summary, when you add your conflicted, fallible, sensual human nature to the mix of life on Earth, your Free Will, and the natural chaos of the Universe, there is a richness of opportunity with humans, for souls, that does not exist anywhere else in all of Creation. There is so much death and physical and emotional hurt, with powerful thoughts attached, that the Planet, the Plane, and the Universe reverberate with them.

Humans simply treat one another and themselves abominably across a wide scale of physical and emotional abuse, crime, corruption, deception, disloyalty, intimidation, you name it. Truly, humanity is the Wild Child of Creation, which almost perfectly suits the Divine One's objective for Learning opportunities.

Almost.

The most important message here about humans is that there is a serious problem with the way they think. And this, of course, affects the way they behave.

Human brains are rooted in the physical plane, but your thoughts, which come from your minds, are at a higher vibration than your bodies are. This is what makes human thoughts more powerful than they should be at your vibration and what makes them so distressing to the rest of Creation. Since Creation is permanently set to default to Love, Hate is abhorrent and relatively rare in the rest of Creation. Remember that hate is the least-necessary emotion in the Universe, but humans on Earth default to it, which sends ripples of Hate throughout Creation. There are some advantages to having thoughts at a higher vibration than the body. This greatly enhances the power of prayer, for example. The downside is what causes so much trouble. Remember that the Universe is a thought-created environment. When humans "create" negative thoughts, these thoughts go streaming outside of your plane in all directions and armies of souls are involved in the "cleanup." In this you all keep the angels very busy as a result of your minds and the powerful thoughts they create as humanity slides up and down the scale of good and bad thoughts. Although human thoughts encompass love, compassion, helpfulness, kindness, and gentleness, hateful thoughts exceed loving thoughts on balance, and therein lies the problem.

Your soul's primary job is to help each of you "get it" and then make better choices. This will reduce and eventually eliminate Hate-filled thoughts. But since most of the souls you generally have as partners are the least experienced they are not all that successful in controlling you. On the other hand this helps them to Learn but here is a key point: *the way humans have developed on Earth has created an organism on an almost permanent downward spiral away from Enlightenment.* This puts you in trouble with the Divine Plan. Under the million monkey theorem, random activity will eventually produce all possible results, which would include what the Divine One intends. If it isn't random, it is determinate, and if it is determinate, then in which direction is it determined to go? Unfortunately, your negative, high-vibration thoughts have shown a distinctively nonrandom pattern. Humans are more often than not displaying determined pro-Hate, anti-Love thoughts, which lead to negative behavior. This is in spite of the fact that soul-partners have always done their best, with varying degrees of success, to steer humans away from wrong thoughts and behavior.

The Divine One gave us all Free Will, but He is hopeful that all humans will eventually row the boat in the right direction—away from Hate and toward Love. Right now, too many are rowing in the wrong direction. To avoid another major course correction—such as another Flood or flood-like apocalypse—humans need to tone down the Hate. The current behavior is indeed "bothering the neighbors" throughout Creation. *This means that vast numbers of entities above the Earth Plane are negatively affected by your constant stream of hateful thoughts, words, and deeds.*

Super-Souls, Compound-Souls, and the more enlightened Simple-Souls among you are engaged in the work to turn around this situation. If they fail, humans can slow the overall march toward Perfection and Reunification or bring it to a halt altogether.

10

THE HUMAN-SOUL PARTNERSHIP

"We have taught ourselves who we think we are. But how often have we allowed who we are to teach us?"

James Blanchard Cisneros

The purpose of this chapter is to clarify the issue surrounding the dual nature of all humans. Everyone reading this is both human and spirit, one physical and mortal and the other non-physical and immortal. What you will get here is more clarity on how the partnership works and what its purpose is.

Souls have existed since the beginning of everything, and what can be classed as remotely human has been around for maybe two million of your years. There has never been a day when humans—from small, early, ape-like animals to modern man—did not have a Spirit or soul to accompany them throughout their lives. Souls have been partnering with living and nonliving things since planets existed. The pond scum that scientists think formed the first identifiable life on Earth was invested with souls, as was everything else. Even dinosaurs had souls. So there should be no notion that humans are uniquely singled out as partners or hosts for souls. There should also be no thought that souls offer the human any choice in the matter, any more than souls offer anything else any choice, be it an oak tree, your desk, or a pigeon. The partnership formed by this union of body and soul enables the human to live with much-needed background guidance and help from its Spirit partner.

> *Narrator: I remember running up a mountain slope as a teenager, and I came to a dead stop at the edge of a sudden cliff face. I had not been looking up, just down at my feet, and did not see the precipice coming. But my soul partner obviously knew it was there and stopped me before I could disappear over the edge. I vividly remember my shock at seeing the drop-off and how I came to a sudden, and unconsciously dead stop in my run up the rocks. I contrast that with what happened to a high school friend years later who was crushed by a falling boulder not many miles from where I was saved. If his soul saw that*

coming, it did nothing to move him out of the way. While I am sad for my friend and his family, I am also curious as to why I was saved and he was not. My Guide tells me it is simply not for me to know, other than our individual journeys are all just that— individual. I also remember another time, in Vietnam, when the pilot of the helicopter I had been in that day tossed some broken pieces of metal onto my desk and said that a post-flight check turned up this little problem. That metal part, he explained, was what allowed a helicopter to achieve blade pitch, which enables the machine to fly. It was in two pieces but did not come off as it should be expected to have done, causing us to crash. We all just shook our heads and wondered at our good fortune. Or was it something else?

Souls are of significant benefit to their human partners, but there is also a benefit that accrues to souls from this partnership. This is because the partnership allows souls to more effectively participate in the Grand Challenge called Reunification. Souls need their human partners to help them understand what humans really go through in their demanding physical and emotional environments. There is simply no other way an energy being can understand what a physical being goes through as it makes choices during every waking hour. The intensity and difficulty of life on Earth come as quite a shock to the souls who experience it for the first of many times. This provides unparalleled experiences and opportunities for the souls who take it on. This difficulty surrounding conflicting desires and needs is essential if the soul is to grow on its own and succeed in helping the human survive while the soul marches toward Enlightenment and Perfection.

Humans are great at all kinds of love with a small "l," but most of you find the Love with a capital "L" as required in the Divine's plan too hard to achieve much of the time. So you are given plenty of help. Your soul partners as well as more advanced souls ride herd on you constantly, but you often don't listen. The difficulty stems from the fact that Free Will must be respected. The hard part is persuading humans to choose the correct path on their own—less Hate and more Love. Here is a key point: Souls are not experts in helping humans get it right. They started out as pure fragments of the Divine, yes, pure but small, ignorant, and immature, and nearly powerless. As they move through the lives of human beings, they fall prey to the vices of their hosts and incur what you could call negative karma from bad choices and poor behavior. Souls must earn their stripes, so to speak, by gradually taking more active control of their hosts to ensure they do good rather than evil. Remember the human default to physical and genetic history: kill or be killed, eat or be eaten, breed early and often to insure the survival of the species. As souls become more adept at controlling their hosts, both the hosts and the souls benefit. There is much less turmoil, uncertainty, enmity, anger, and, yes, much less of the *Bête Noir* of the Universe—Hate. Simply stated, humans with more advanced, merged souls as their partners do much better in life. Humans with immature souls as partners do not do as well but provide a richer Learning environment. You only have to look around to see who may have the more advanced soul partners.

People think folks who demonstrate great initiative, great talent, or great genius are "gifted," and indeed they are. They are gifted with souls that are more advanced than average, which means they are growing in their understanding of the Divine Plan and have more control over their human partners. *Humans, therefore, need their soul partners to help them survive as individuals and as a race, while souls need their human partners in order to intensify their Learning process.*

Because it's natural for you to wonder who is in charge, the human or the soul, the answer is that they both are. Think of the old saying, "A devil on one shoulder and an angel on the other". The human has motivations based on the five senses and the imperative for survival. Do I fight or do I run? Does it feel good? Does it taste good? Will we have healthy babies? And their emotions. Will it make me more attractive? Will it give me more power? Will I win the lottery? The soul, on the other hand, has far different motives for choosing any course of action. How does this affect others? Is it in accordance with the reason I am here? Will it further The Divine One's Plan? So essentially the devil on your left shoulder is the human side of you—passionate, pleasure-seeking, pain-avoiding, survival-of-the-fittest, damn the torpedoes, full speed ahead. The angel on your right shoulder is your soul, which is more interested in longer-term, nonsensual goals. Whatever the human does, regardless of who influenced or made the decision, will affect both human and soul, and those around them. This is the way things are intended. That is the whole point behind chaos-generating Free Will.

The reason this is important to understand is that humans, as currently developed, are, if left to their own devices, on a perpetually downward spiral of behavior. This interferes with the Divine Plan of Reunification. Left to their own devices, humans won't ever Learn to abandon Hate totally and adopt Love totally. It is therefore the task of souls to help humanity survive its own nature in order to further the Divine Plan. The soul, in turn, Learns how hard it is to stay on the straight and narrow on the oh-so-sensual physical plane.

Everyone reading this is an energy being, an immortal soul, a fragment of the Creator, who has been offered and accepted the invitation to experience physical life in order to Learn. You are all, of course, also human beings. The two are inseparable, even if they are not one and the same. They can't be the same. One dies, while the other does not.

11

THE DIVINE IN EACH OF YOU

*"My God's not dead, He's surely alive,
He's living on the inside."*

**From the song God's Not Dead,
by The Newsboys**

An important objective of this chapter is to help you understand, among other things, what is meant by the phrase "tap into the Divine within you." It is important to understand that you have at your core a fragment of the Divine Himself. This is your soul. It's therefore not only possible to use the Divine within you; it's also mandatory. It's an obligation. Your Creator has given you the ultimate gift: a bit of Himself. This gift is not to be squandered or ignored. It is to be used to advance your Creator's objective—Reunification.

So you aren't there just to sip double-tall no-foam skinny lattes. Nor are you there just to be brutally murdered by someone or to be a killer yourself, although all options are on the table. Your purpose behind the permission you were given to be there in physical form requires more than getting up in the morning and pursuing your day. You must be an active participant in pursuit of your spiritual goals. Call it your destiny, if you prefer. To do that, you need to recognize and grab hold of the Divine within you, feel the energy it has, and use it properly. If you can do that, then you can achieve your purpose on Earth and move that much closer to Enlightenment and then Perfection, which brings us all that much closer to Reunification.

SECTION FIVE

The Meaning of Life

12

THE MEANING OF LIFE

"It does not matter how long you are spending on the earth, how much money you have gathered, or how much attention you have received. It is the amount of positive vibration you have radiated in life that matters."

Amit Ray

Here is the meaning of life: **your task, no matter how many lives it takes, is to Learn to abandon Hate in favor of Love and demonstrate that you have done so by your thoughts, words, and deeds.** This is your individual spiritual path and the process that achieves the Divine One's Reunification.

There is of course a difference between experiencing and Learning. You can witness every sort of good and bad act and do every sort of good and bad act, but that does not imply that you have learned anything from them. And what, you may ask, are you supposed to Learn? Simply stated, you are there to Learn to embrace Love and to abandon Hate. Learning in this context, that is the context of the Divine Plan for Reunification, is not the same kind of everyday learning you do in school or in your family or on the job. This is Learning with a capital "L." It is a fundamental part of the Universe and a pretext for Reunification. It is on par with Free Will and completely related to it. Learning while exercising Free Will is pretty much the only prerequisite for the testing you undergo all day, every day.

So the lesson for you now is to realize that you need to pay a great deal more attention to your actions while striving to be your best regardless of the circumstances. As souls continue their march toward Enlightenment and Perfection, they participate in the unfolding of events resulting from their partnerships with their human hosts. What they are not able to grasp while on Earth are ripples and echoes to and from the vastness of everywhere else. Throughout your many lives on the Earth Plane, you remain connected to all of them, in each of them, although mostly not consciously. Every now and then, you run across people and places that trigger distant memories. You call these moments *déjà vu* and usually let them pass. Some people go to psychic readers who can connect them with past lives, but the greater part of humanity is oblivious to connections with former lives. That is actually perfectly fine and does not interfere with the objective of your current life, which is to advance your soul's spiritual journey by improving its ability to Learn, Grow, Understand, and finally Control certain aspects of Divine Energy.

In your many journeys and experiences on Earth or elsewhere on the physical plane, you will work hard and be lazy. You will be rich and poor. You will be healthy and sickly. You will be intelligent and dim-witted. You will be brave and cowardly. You will be fat and thin. You will be artistic and not so much. You will do great things and not-so-great things. You will help your family, and you will be nothing but a burden. You will keep doing these things, and more, until you understand that the path to Reunification goes through Enlightenment and Perfection. Advancing along that path requires that you Learn to completely discard Hate as an option and adopt Love as your only mode of behavior. Once you reach that state of Perfection, you will no longer cause unnecessary pain and suffering to yourself, to other people, to animals, or to anything else. Bottom line: *Learning, with a capital "L," is coming to the absolute realization, belief, and practice that there is nothing more fundamental to understanding and being "One with God" than Love*—in every fiber of your being—as evidenced by your thoughts, words, and deeds.

Every act you have decided to do—big or little, good or bad—has come with consequences. These actions, which begin with thoughts, have required choices of some kind, and it is in your choices where your level of understanding of Hate versus Love is assessed. Where are you in your march toward Enlightenment and Perfection? The answer determines how much more and what kind of Learning you need to do.

The effects of your choices on others is as important as the effects of your choices on yourself. Which of your actions helped others and yourself Learn something positive? Did any of your thoughts, words, or deeds help move things forward or backward? Did any of your actions help you or others to Learn?

The very essence of your existence on Earth is to Learn what the Divine One, in His infinite wisdom, wants you to Learn. *You are there for yourself, but it is important to remember that you are not by yourself.* You live on a planet with some seven billion other people who are also there to Learn. It is also important to remember that it is not just people you are there to Learn with. There are animals, plants, insects, microbes, and such, all of whom are conscious and all of whom are valuable parts of the Learning process. Every one of those beings is hosting a soul on the same mission to Learn that you have. You all have Free Will, and the resulting interactive chaos you create is exactly what is intended and what you need. If you can demonstrate that you have learned the ultimate lesson—with all the chaos of free choice, with all the temptations you face, with no other Divine law except Free Will—then, you have Learned what you have been charged with learning.

The course set before you therefore, is extremely difficult. You are bound to the intensity of human nature and the real dangers of life on Earth. Because you have total freedom to choose any course of action you desire, there is an inherent conflict of choice. Do you choose pleasure for yourself or pain? Do you choose pleasure for others or pain? Do you do physical harm or physical good? Do you do emotional harm or emotional good? There are of course constraints on all behavior because of human laws, rules, societal pressures, family influences, and self-control. In spite of that, you, as part of the human race, find it all too easy to do as you please, which includes giving in to Hate and doing things that cause more Hate. The resulting human behavior is great for Learning, but choosing to be obstinate and unloving under Free Will is not good if it's a permanent condition.

You need to be crystal clear on this point because it is the absolute bottom line to Why You Are there. *The Divine One's intention is for everyone to get to the point where the sum total of everything that defines any and all of you is Love. This means that by definition there is no Hate in your souls whatsoever.* That is everybody's goal, because the desired end state for Everything is that all energy is Love. At that point, the Big Bang becomes the Big Reunification. So do whatever you want, but Learn from it. And in so doing, begin walking the correct path.

13

CLARIFYING AND REINFORCING THE PROCESS OF LEARNING

"'Cause every hand's a winner and every hand's a loser and the best that you can hope for is to die in your sleep."

From The Gambler *by Kenny Rogers*

As a consequence of its suspicious, survival orientation, the human animal constantly challenges and even attacks its spiritual core. This is one of the conditions you face: intense Learning is made possible by the chaos of Free Will as well as the constant pressure of your human partners to provide every impediment possible to climbing out of the sometimes anti-spiritual ooze you live in on Earth. Lust, greed, jealousy, disease, famine, beatings, murder, and rape are all options. Depending on the life that you and your Guides have chosen for you, these things can come more or less often. This manifests in a variety of ways, but know this: the devil and all the many hosts of scary things that go bump in the night are wholly created by your human imaginations (thoughts) and because it is the nature of the human hosts to make this happen. No matter how enlightened your human partner, no matter how gentle your condition, your partner will never be totally content and will find ways to give your soul ample temptation to sway you from your goal.

The resulting chaos and general unpredictability of life for souls on your plane is essential to the overall Plan. You might be thinking that the task set before you in this "game" of Reunification is too hard, but from our Creator's point of view, His Plan could not be any more elegant or work any other way. Each conscious fragment of the Divine—that's you and me and every other soul—regardless of where we are on our spiritual journeys, is free to do anything at all. It is this very freedom that results in random behavior that allows many mistakes to be made and much Learning to be achieved, at least eventually. Ignorant freedom like that on Earth is the most intense and desired. It is ignorant because you do not remember exactly why you have been sent there, and you tend to forget the grand scheme—that there is a Creator who has expectations of you. You do not remember exactly what you are to Learn, but this ignorance is essential. If you can get it right while ignorant of your Learning objective in any given lifetime, while distracted by the most physically sensate place in the Universe and while partnering with the most advanced thinking-sensory beings in all of Creation (humans), you will have achieved Learning effectively and beneficially. Living on Earth is therefore, for the soul, sort of like sports training at high altitudes. It provides a more intense set of adversities. If you knew why you were there this time, your choices under that adversity would not be made honestly. It's like copying somebody else's exam in school. That is no way to prove you know the answers, only that you can read and write. So you must make your choices in life while buffeted by the many conflicting emotions and sensory temptations that exist for humans. If you can make the right choices and persuade your human partner to follow suit under these difficult circumstances, then you can demonstrate that you understand and accept the "correct" choices to make.

The bottom line is what lyrics from *The Gambler* are saying: life is what you make of it, so play the cards you're dealt as best you can. Your life is filled with opportunities to do much or little, good or bad. Since you are there in your ignorant and human state, there is every likelihood that you will often make the wrong choices. In the end, the choices you make either prove you "get it" or prove you don't, at least not yet. When you don't get it, you get to do it over again.

14

THE CONDITIONS UNDER WHICH YOU LEARN ARE ESSENTIAL

How The Universe Works

> *"Two things are infinite: the universe and human stupidity, and I'm not sure about the universe."*
>
> *Albert Einstein*

There are many things about The Universe as a whole that you can't experience at your physical vibration and that you don't need to know about. Remember, most of the Universe is outside the physical planes. It is important, however, for you to have some understanding or awareness of The Universe so you can more easily understand the part you play in it. Energy is the key to understanding it all but there is no way you can fully understand all that the word "Energy" entails here since it has many more applications in the Universe at large than it does there on your physical plane.

In terms you can understand, the Universe is designed to enable, but not guarantee, Reunification. This means that Reunification might not happen but under the million monkey theorem, Reunification should happen, eventually. According to the theorem, random activity will produce every possible outcome. That is what our Creator is determined to find out, but is all the chaos produced by conscious fragments of the Divine random? Is human behavior, for example, random or determinate?

Everything that happens on every plane leaves "ripples in the pond" of the Universe. This includes all of Creation, most of which is nonphysical, and all physical parts of the Universe, which is what you can experience with your five human senses. The expansion and contraction of steel in a bridge, the settling and erosion of every grain of sand in the deserts and in the oceans, the melting of every drop of winter snow, the splitting of every atom in every star, the energy that connects everything with everything else, all your thoughts and prayers and curses and hatreds and loves and acts of courage, and acts cowardice and cruelty, ad infinitum, are felt in one way or another throughout Creation. The Creator experiences all of it in real time and for all time. That was how He designed it before setting it into motion.

As all this happens, has happened, and will happen, certain chains of events from all this physical and non-physical activity affect the process of Reunification. You can never know what the full ripple effect is throughout your own societies, much less The Universe, from the thoughts, words, and deeds you do. With seven billion people on Earth, the interconnectedness you have with the events of your daily lives is immense and complex. All day, every day, you face choices. It is in these choices, some simple some highly complex, that you have opportunities to demonstrate your level of Learning. Because human activity on Earth ripples out into the rest of the Universe, within the physical planes and also into the energy planes, humans are a noisy bunch, mostly because your brains produce thoughts above your own vibration, which makes them more transferable to the energy planes than other things in the "mud layer" of your physical existence. Remember this: *your brain is locked into the Physical Plane, but your mind is not, and the thoughts it creates affect all of Creation.*

Many souls, operating on their own Free Will, are working hard to help realize the Divine One's goal of Reunification. You and I are part of this army of souls doing what we can to achieve it—or not. Tied as souls are to human bodies and therefore human nature, and because so many souls are still small, inexperienced, weak, and immature, too many Earthbound souls seem hell-bent on following their human hosts in the wrong direction. Not only that, human thoughts and actions affect more than just your planet and your Plane. Because of the powerful nature of human thought, the waves of palpable hate you broadcast into the Universe act like a drag chute on the process of Reunification. Remember that Reunification is the process by which the Divine One is put back together, which is achieved only when every conscious fragment "gets it" and abandons Hate in favor of Love.

The Sanctity of Life
A key to understanding how so much troublesome stuff can be going on in the world is this: *your physical life is not sacred, but what you do with it is.*

Your human life matters considerably, but not for the reason you might think. What matters is your purpose for being where you are right now, with that family, with that job and other activities, with those people, and with your soul as a partner. Being there is simply a context for what your soul is supposed to do with all the opportunities it has to make right and wrong choices—in partnership with the human. To the Divine, a human body is important but no more important than a tree. Both are vessels for souls. Add to that the fact that while unique in all of Creation, humans are troublesome vessels and trees are not. The bottom line is that your life now, and all previous and future physical lives, are not sacred—important, yes, but not sacred. What you are supposed to do with those lives is sacred. This distinction may seem nuanced, but it is the key to understanding the Meaning of Life.

Your physical life is not sacred. What you do with it is.
Your soul is an immortal being that matters forever. Your current human life matters insofar as you have been allowed to experience it, briefly, with your soul as its partner, and to make the best of it while you have it. Good and bad things happen to everyone, and the sum total of all your experiences and the choices you make along the way are part of your continuing struggle to Get Right with the Divine One's overall plan. The situation into which you were born was thought to provide the best opportunity to Learn what you needed to Learn this time. If a building fell on you as a child or if you were kidnapped and tortured and murdered—bad as that is—it is part of being there. Learn from it, and move on. "You" do not really die anyway. Your body dies at some point, and then you get another one.

Good and Evil, Love and Hate

> *"What if evil doesn't really exist? What if evil is something dreamed up by man, and there is nothing to struggle against except our own limitations? The constant battle between our will, our desires, and our choices?"*
>
> *Libba Bray*

"A Native American elder once described his own inner struggles in this manner: 'Inside of me there are two dogs. One of the dogs is mean and evil. The other dog is good. The mean dog fights the good dog all the time.' When asked which dog wins, he reflected for a moment and replied, the one I feed the most."

George Bernard Shaw

Good, evil, love, and hate are all thoughts. Those labels can also be applied to actions, but they begin as creations of the mind and are therefore powerful in the thought-created environment just above and beyond your physical plane. Hate is the least necessary of all emotions and energies, but it is on the Physical Planes—especially on Earth—and within the human heart, that hate thrives. It is your duty to conquer Hate, but Free Will and the seductive nature of physical life in your amazing human body result in powerful temptations and choices to do otherwise. This creates conflicts between and among all people and groups of people all the time. This is great for Learning but only if you actually Learn from it.

Good and evil are not separate. They are just opposite sides of your human nature. Without evil or hate, doing good or being good would be the only choice, so there would be nothing to Learn about choice. Individual souls have so much to Learn in order to move toward Enlightenment and Perfection and Reunification. The human experience on Earth is the most challenging and therefore the most effective training and Learning place in all of Creation. Humans are constantly caught up in agony of choices on the physical plane. At the point where you are no longer at odds with the best of yourself and are no longer capable of evil or hatred, you have Learned the final lesson. Some would say you have achieved Enlightenment at that point and are free of the need to live on Earth or anywhere else on the physical plane. As a human on Earth, especially, this is easy to say and not so easy to do given the sensory nature of your world and of humankind. The chaos that is the natural order of things gives you so many opportunities to make the wrong choices. Humans rationalize and invent convenient constructs such as "situational ethics" that insinuate permission to do what they know to be wrong just because "everyone else does it." They dig holes for themselves and spend lifetimes trying to climb out of these holes. And that is precisely the way it is supposed to be.

> *Narrator: I remember vividly the scenes in the* Ghostbusters *movies where what they called ectoplasmic slime responds to the hate of those around it and multiplies, fills the storm drains, and eventually covers an entire*

> *building in New York City. There is no doubt in my mind that whoever wrote that script was tapped into the same truth I am laying out here, whether they realized it or not. Hate is the opposite of Love. It is powerful, it is compelling, it is tangible, and it is something we humans are excellent at creating. Love, on the other hand, while it conquers Hate, as it did in* Ghostbusters, *is far more difficult for too many humans to produce as easily or as often as its opposite.*

You are supposed to struggle against your physical dangers and relationships with others and conquer the worst side of yourself in the process of Learning. The problems you encounter along the way provide opportunities to Learn what you are there to Learn. As you struggle throughout your life, you follow an understandable survival imperative. As part of this imperative, which developed as you did in a kill-or-be-killed, eat-or-be-eaten, breed-or-face-extinction physical environment, you came to know both love and hate, among other emotions. The problem the Universe has with humanity is the way it so easily and powerfully expresses hate and its various related emotions, such as anger. You should know, though, that hate does not exist naturally throughout the Universe. So why does it exist on Earth? It's simple, really. You create it. You think it. And this matters to all of Creation because you live in a thought-created Universe even if you are somewhat circumscribed in its use. In your dangerous physical environment, it is natural and good for your survival to fear certain things. Unfortunately, things that make you afraid can also give rise to a sister emotion called anger, which is one of the manifestations of Hate, the *bête noir* of the Universe. When you were a child and feared a monster under your bed, the monster was as real as your thoughts, and your fears created it. When you didn't think of it, it didn't exist. When you thought of it, you got goose bumps from the fear it created in you. Nobody else in the house was affected by the monster because it was in *your* thoughts, not theirs. When you shared these thoughts with others, they would smile and sympathize or pooh-pooh them but were not bothered by them as you were. So it's an interesting problem our Creator has set for you: *create evil in order to defeat it*

Hate is in and of itself a destructive energy, but because you create it, you also can eliminate it. The enduring problem you face in this regard is that hate is such an easy emotion to conjure that you create it willy-nilly throughout your waking hours and even in your dreams. It costs nothing and can be weirdly satisfying when you get caught up in it. Somebody cuts in front of you in a line. You momentarily hate that person and maybe even start a confrontation. At that point, the person hates you, and so on throughout your days and your lives. Defeating Hate and its attendant emotions may seem to be a hard task, but you can conquer your predilection toward hatred. You can calm yourself. It is as simple as thinking nicer thoughts. But will you do it, and when? Those are the important questions confronting humanity and your many Guides.

Pain and Suffering

> *"Life is a 'valley of tears,' a period of trial and suffering, an unpleasant but necessary preparation for the afterlife where alone man could expect to enjoy happiness."*
>
> *Archibald T. McAllister*
>
> *"Out of suffering have emerged the strongest souls; the most massive characters are seared with scars."*
>
> *Kahlil Gibran*

The pain and suffering of the Human Condition has been much addressed throughout history, but a more focused read on pain and suffering can be instructive. Everyone at some time or other has wondered how the Divine One can allow so much suffering in the world. As with all "big" questions, the answer is deceptively simple: you must endure all possible experiences, including great joy and great suffering, in order to Learn to make the best possible choices. Once you understand that human lives are important to our Creator only for soul journeys, and are not in and of themselves sacred, then perhaps you can see how pain and suffering are allowable. Once you understand this, then the veil may be lifted a bit on why really bad things happen even to good people, or to animals, or to the planet.

As a practical matter, the Learning environment on Earth is one in which everything that has happened is allowed to happen, including all the things that happen to people. This is important: *everything that happens is allowed to happen.* To be sure, most things are "allowed" by default, given your Free Will and given what you are capable of doing. There is no intervention in these affairs. It is pointless to speculate on what is and is not allowed to happen, every day, and why. You need to know only that the priorities in play from a Divine perspective are considerably different from your own.

> *Narrator: According to a quick fact check on the Internet, the wars and atrocities of just the twentieth century, representing direct or indirect deaths of human beings by other human beings, accounted for 195 million dead. That is a little more than the current population of Brazil. Unbelievable. Super-Souls can stop anything from happening, and they have unlimited access and methods for doing so. So you look at history and see that the Holocaust*

> *was allowed. The world wars of the twentieth century were allowed. The Killing Fields in Cambodia were allowed. The brutal civil wars in Africa were allowed. The terrorist attacks on 9/11/2001 were allowed. Terrorism in general is allowed. Going farther back, the Crusades were allowed. The Inquisition was allowed. The devastation of the Native American civilizations, both north and south, was allowed. So many events on such a massive scale of destruction and pain and suffering—all allowed. We can only sit and wonder what evil we humans have dreamed up that was not allowed.*

During the span of your soul's many incarnations in physical human life, you will be murderers and the murdered. You will be sinners and saints. You will be male and female, all races, all persuasions, rich and poor, smart and not so smart, physically healthy and physically challenged, powerful in one incarnation and weak in another, and everything in between. This is necessary in order for you to be fully tested against the standard of abandoning Hate and accepting only Love under every possible circumstance. If everyone were beautiful and rich and powerful and kind all the time, how challenging would life on Earth be? What would there be to Learn? How would Reunification take place? Chaotic lives are not punishment; they are opportunities for growth. They provide situations where adversity can be used to the Divine's advantage and not wasted. You must honor your commitment and your obligation to further the Divine One's Plan, and you cannot achieve this by living a single life or even many lives. This is not a quantity thing, but instead is a quality thing. You achieve success in your spiritual journey by living each life better than the one before it and by remembering that Hate in its many forms and manifestations is to be avoided and discarded at every opportunity. When you are ready and Love is to be welcomed and adopted as your only feeling, then you move toward Enlightenment, Perfection, and Reunification.

So please understand that regardless of what life brings to you, good and bad, you are supposed to deal with it as best you can and eventually, after many, many attempts, conquer all temptations you face by defaulting to Love, not Hate, as a response. This must be seen as not suffering nor joy, but rather as valuable experiences that give you the best chance to Learn the ultimate lesson. So at the bottom of all places in Creation, you are a student of what it means to live in physical form. Smell the smells. See the sights. Have the passions. Feel, taste, hear, experience the senses individually and collectively. Help others. Hurt others. Heal the sick. Spread disease. Be a caregiver. Love. Laugh. Cry. Die. Over and over again until you have sufficient Experience to knit it all together and start making more informed choices about what it means to live up to your potential and achieve Enlightenment and then Perfection. This is the only process available as your soul develops and matures on its way to Reunification.

How many lives does this take? There is no set number. For each soul, it is simply a matter of getting it done. At some point in the journey, you become aware that there is more to your life than physical torments and pleasures. Religions and laws are commonly reflective of and incorporate this recognition, but because you have free choice, you find an enormous diversity of opinion as to the proper way to behave and the consequences of bad behavior. And once again, you fall back into the arsenal of physical, sensual passions and even use religion as pretext for more suffering. What rich Learning environments the Inquisitions and the Crusades were!

So your "life" is essentially a school with your human partners with Earth as your classroom. With now some seven billion humans on Earth, all with the same purpose and all interacting with one another with no Divine rules other than doing whatever they want to do, there is so much chaos and therefore so much opportunity to make your choices, good or bad, and thereby to Learn. As you Learn, you gain awareness of the larger picture and make better choices and eventually "get it," and then get it right, and then rejoin your Creator. When this happens, The Divine One achieves what He has set out to do, having observed and experienced so many things from each of His fragments. As you suffered or experienced joy, The Divine One suffered and experienced joy with you and with millions and billions of other of His conscious energy fragments, all the time. In this way, the Divine One Learns too. The Divine One knows everything, but with Free Will distributed among His own fragments, a large measure of independent action and unpredictability is present. It is from this unpredictability that The Divine One Learns while you Learn. So does The Divine One care that babies are suffering? Yes, but not in the way you care. The Divine One did not mandate the suffering exactly but did create the potential for it by establishing Free Will, and this made suffering inevitable. From a human perspective, it is your own nature that causes so much suffering in the world. These are humankind's self-inflicted wounds and well within the master plan of the Universe. So as you die a terrible death and pray for the Divine One to intervene, remember that your Creator Loves you, but also remember who and what your body and soul are to your God. *Even as your physical body suffers and dies, your soul is an undying part of the Divine providing richness to the tapestry of His Existence.*

Divine Intervention

"The universe is like a river. The river keeps on flowing. It doesn't care whether you are happy or sad, good or bad; it just

> *keeps flowing. Some people go down to the river and they cry. Some people go down to the river and they are happy, but the river doesn't care; it just keeps flowing. We can use it and enjoy it, or we can jump in and drown. The river just keeps flowing because it is impersonal, and so it is with the universe. The universe that we live in can support us or destroy us. It's our interpretation and use of its laws that determine our effects or results."*
>
> *Robert Anthony*

To understand the true nature of Divine intervention, you need to remember that following the Prime Intervention, that is, the Big Bang, and the resulting creation of the Universe, the Divine One became essentially noninterventionist on a personal level. That was His whole Plan: to Create a Universe where chaos is the order of the day for any conscious thing that can make a choice, (us souls), and let things follow their own course with an eye toward His intended result. That said, Divine intervention is not only possible, but it does happen.

Divine intervention takes many forms. For example, your soul is a form of Divine intervention. Each soul does its best to rein in the baser instincts of its human partner so it might have a ghost of a chance to fulfill the Divine Plan. And because of human nature, you keep the angels busy riding herd on things that interfere with the Plan. They intervene when appropriate as determined by the Angels themselves, not the Divine One directly. Remember, things that work against Reunification go against the Divine Plan. For this reason, there have been, and continue to be, "course corrections", designed to help you move forward in spite of yourselves. The great dinosaur die-off, and the Flood, for example, were two such "corrections," as were the lives of Jesus, Muhammad, and Buddha, among others. The dinosaurs and other living creatures that would have made it too difficult for humans to thrive had to go. The Flood was a correction that drastically reduced a human population that was absolutely wrong for the Divine Plan but which had only limited effect. When the water subsided, things simply continued as before. The life of Christ was a more effective approach, leaving humanity with lessons of Love, forgiveness, and compassion that still resonate. This gave proof of the power of an idea—a thought, after all. To the life and lessons of Christ, we can add the lives and interventions of other great prophets, saints, and other holy people, as well as nice, simple people who may live next door to you or work with you and have positive influences on your life. Earth and the human experience provide such a great Learning environment that souls are lined up to go there, and, yes, there is a waiting list of sorts.

So while the Divine One does not get involved in your life directly, there is plenty of Divine help, or intervention, from more advanced souls. They are working on their own initiative to push the Divine Plan forward, bearing in mind that Free Will is not to be interfered with because that goes against the basic conditions for Creation this time around.

Remember that all souls are immortal fragments of the Divine One. And remember that all of us at whatever stage of maturity have the same mission: to assist reunification through the attainment of Enlightenment and then Perfection by Learning to abandon Hate in favor of Love. The "reward" for achieving Enlightenment and Perfection is the *merger of like-achieving souls*. Remember the example of how liquid mercury can break up into many tiny droplets? That was like the Big Bang. Our Creator fragmented into all of what exists throughout Creation. Our souls are like those drops of mercury, sloshing around as they go about their quest for Enlightenment and Perfection. When they achieve it, they merge with other Enlightened and Perfected "droplets." So these larger combined fragments of The Divine One have more Divine Energy and Awareness and have more Divine Power and Responsibilities.

Perfected entities of great magnitude, or major Super-Souls like the one that incarnated in the body of Jesus Christ, are capable of bridging the gap between the spiritual planes and the physical planes.

This gives them the ability to establish thought creation on Earth. Changing water into wine or healing the sick is as simple to a Super-Soul of great magnitude as just thinking that it be so.

Jesus Christ provided Earth with a well-known example of Divine intervention and the power of advanced, great-magnitude Super-Souls. Powerful agents of The Divine decided that things were sliding in the wrong direction again (after the Flood). Because the problem was greater than just too many people, a different approach was used. A remarkable Man was provided to humankind as an example of what direction to take in life. The miracles ascribed to Jesus were the work of the Super-Soul partner to the body of Christ, who had the power and the authority to show His divine nature through the public work of miracles and through preaching a different religious message: *one of love and forgiveness instead of hate and retribution.* Jesus took the task of spreading a gospel of peace and love at a time when there was very little of that in evidence on Earth, the ground zero of the five senses, where sensual tension pushes many humans away from Love with a capital "L." The story and lessons of Jesus are so powerful that they continue to spread to this day. The Divine One's story was told through Jesus, and later through his disciples and the adherents of what became Christianity, although many religions have at their core the same correct message.

Christ is the embodiment of the Perfection that the Divine One intends for all souls. His physical body suffered and died for humanity, but, more important, He gave a powerful message of hope and love and compassion that endures after thousands of years. The life of Christ is not unique. The same objective, saving humanity from itself, can be applied to all the religious miracles and teaching of love and compassion by holy men and women of all faiths throughout human history and around the world. These things continue to happen because they are done by powerful souls who are furthering the Divine One's overall objective of Reunification. There is also casual evidence of Divine intervention on a much broader but much less dramatic scale than the life of Jesus or even the lives of saints. Visitors to holy shrines around the world will attest to this.

> *Narrator: Closer to home, my wife and I were casual witnesses to one such Intervention. My wife, who is a talented medium and psychic, saw an Angel appear at an intersection immediately before two cars were on a course to collide. All I saw was one car swerve at the last split second to avoid the accident, while the other one hit the brakes. What my wife saw was a glowing white, twenty-foot-tall winged human hand that she called an angel, or part of an angel, suddenly appear in the intersection. This angel put its hand out toward the car that veered away. As soon*

as the danger passed, the Angel faded from my wife's view. Amazing. I wondered what it was about these two cars, the people in them, and the people around them that caused this Divine intervention, but I understand that it is not for me to know or guess as to the reason this accident was prevented. It's not totally implausible that it was done so I would see it and put it in this narrative. Who knows? On one hand, we can be glad that The Divine One enables some assistance to us, but we are left wondering why situations like the Holocaust or the Killing Fields are not prevented. I have no idea what the threshold for Divine intervention is. Seemingly, the car crash that was averted is small compared with the Holocaust, so there is obviously more to this than the sheer magnitude of the events when The Divine One's agents intervene.

It all gets back to humanity's need for opportunities to Learn from your mistakes during the lives you live there. What amazing Learning opportunities are available during situations like World War II or the Cambodian Killing Fields. During every waking moment by everyone affected by these conflicts, soldiers and civilians alike, there were opportunities to do good and evil, to Love and to Hate. Because you are there to learn to abandon Hate in favor of Love, the power of your Earthly "classroom" environment is obvious, especially during times when great Hate is abroad in the world. There are too many people involved in perverting religion, nationalism, and narcissism to justify their hostile actions, and way too few saintly people like Mother Teresa to hold back the tide. Dropping bombs on people is simply a hateful expedient because it can't kill their ideas. To do that, you need a more compelling idea. That was what the life of Christ was all about. His idea was to Love, not Hate, and show it by turning the other cheek if it came to that. His life and His example have served many well as they struggle to moderate their human behaviors. But look around and you will see that not everyone has bought into the philosophy of Christ or other moderate voices. Consider this: *if the problems of the world could be solved by violence, they would have been solved by now given the amount of violence throughout all of human history.* Try a little tenderness instead.

SECTION SIX

What Happens When You "Die"

15

HEAVEN AND HELL

"Ends are not bad things; they just mean that something else is about to begin. And there are many things that don't really end, anyway; they just begin again in a new way. Ends are not bad and many ends aren't really an ending; some things are never-ending."

C. JoyBell C.

Since all humans face certain death everyone wants to know what happens when they die. You recognize from an early age that your human days are numbered and that, barring accidents or the onset of a deadly disease, older people will die before you do and eventually it is your turn to go. This includes your parents, and in spite of a lifetime of preparation, the loss of a parent is a traumatic event. But what happens to Mom and Dad when they die? Where do they go, and what do they do? Or do they just die and that's that?

The truth is that the physical body after death is simply a conglomeration of liquids and solids and will eventually decompose or is cremated, but there is no consciousness or life beyond death for the physical remains.

Your soul, on the other hand, leaves the body and the physical plane when the host, the human partner, dies. Souls resume their natural state as pure energy beings without physical substance. A soul does retain memories of this life and of all its previous lives and can, when communicating with former family and other acquaintances, both on the physical planes and the spirit planes, assume the appearance of its former human partner if it wishes. It requires only the thought to make that happen.

Passing from physically partnered to purely Spirit is traumatic even for souls that have made the transition many times. There is a period of adjustment during this transition that helps acclimate the soul to its higher vibration. The longer a soul is partnered at the physical vibration, the more adjustment is needed to fully refresh itself to the higher vibrations of the non-physical, spiritual planes. This adjustment, especially immediately after the death of the human partner, is often helped along by the souls of beloved former family members who have already passed. In cases where death is sudden and unexpected, there can be an even longer period of adjustment. The soul must understand that it is no longer partnered with a human host. This adjustment takes no time at all in the spirit planes, where there is no such thing as time, but it can be many, many Earth years before the soul realizes it has "died" as a physical being and needs to move "into the Light," so to speak, of pure Spirit.

When crossing into Spirit, it is necessary to transition through a "place," much like a halfway house, where most souls go. The popular human name for this place is Heaven. Although it is pleasant, it is nothing like the heaven people pray for and long to see someday. It is where your life is reviewed and judged and where decisions are made as to the best next move for you in your Spiritual Journey.

For a few souls, there is an "in-between place" that resembles the Hell that many cultures recognize as a place of punishment. This place is populated by two categories of souls. First are the souls who have passed but identify too closely with their physical lives and are unwilling to give them up. Many of these souls simply enjoyed their debauchery too much, were involved in all manner of atrocities or sensual vices, and reveled in their human power over others. They "think" that is where they should go and because they are in a thought created environment, that's where they are. All the vices are well represented in this "hell." It is not a permanent stop for souls but may seem so in a place where there is no time to measure against. To people leaving the physical planes, it would seem "forever" by the earthly understanding of time. The second category of souls who populate this place are those who feel so guilty over their lives that when they pass they head immediately to this place of depravity for the punishment they feel they so richly deserve. Once again, they "think" that is where they should go and so they do. The first category of what you might call wicked souls are only too happy to provide punishment to souls who want to be punished. While there is no such thing there as physical pain or suffering, it still manifests itself because it is a thought-created environment. Any soul who "thinks" it is in pain and suffering gets its wish in exactly the way it thinks it should be. The scenes depicting *Dante's Inferno* in human art accurately capture the essence of this in-between place. When the time is right for these souls, they are retrieved by their Guides and put into the process of review and judgment before deciding what they will do in the next iteration of their journeys.

> *Narrator: I hesitate to include this next paragraph because it comes from personal experience and not from this Spirit, but it is important as a way to clarify the nature of the "Heaven" you want to expect upon passing into spirit. Several years ago, my wife and I were privileged to visit the place we go after*

we die. We have all been there after past lives, but my wife and I were able to experience it in this life. We didn't die, of course, but we visited it during guided meditations over six weeks of instruction and tours. We first shielded ourselves against the stronger and faster vibrations one level up from this physical plane. We were then taken, in meditation, to the "bridge" between the two worlds and beyond it into the vast complex of compartments where souls are "debriefed" after life on the Earth plane. I will relate the most amazing and strongest of my experiences during one such visit. I was standing by the entrance to the bridge between worlds, and there was a line of recently departed souls making their way across it. They appeared as if in an impressionist painting: indistinct visions of human bodies with no clear details. One such soul, not four feet away from where I was standing, was covered with what looked like a thick shell of black material, which began to fall away in large chunks. I watched in fascination as this happened. At some level, I understood that the soul was shedding itself of all the fears, torments, pain, stress, responsibilities, and sorrows of its life on Earth. I will never forget the wave of overwhelming relief and joy that swept over me from the soul as it rid itself of all its baggage from life on Earth, and as it transitioned to its eternal life as pure Spirit. I realized I was sharing a powerful moment with this soul and sharing its feelings as well as they washed over me. It was an unbelievable, unforgettable experience and certainly was not something I had anticipated before our meditative journey began. In retrospect, I think I was shown that in order that I might share it with you all now. That memory is as vivid today as it was when it happened and has certainly helped me in my own natural struggle with the fear of dying. I now know there is nothing to fear about this at all. I may regret dying but I will not fear it.

16

JUDGMENT

Reflection and Remorse

"If a man has beheld evil, he may know that it was shown to him in order that he may repent, for what is shown to him is also within him."

Rabbi Israel Baal Shem Tov

Everyone involved in physical lives will eventually go through the same process when they pass into Spirit. All souls have reflections and remorse as a result of each thought, word, or deed they consider inappropriate, hurtful, or harmful. On reflection, and as a part of the process of remorse, each soul reaches out to the soul of any and all persons they feel they wronged in some way during their human partnership. Imagine how vast a process this is and how richly rewarding it is as every moment of your life falls under the spotlight of intense review by you and your Guides and as you begin to atone for your mistakes. Any thought, word, or deed that does not measure up to the criteria of abandoning Hate in favor of Love is dealt with critically during this process.

The underlying truth is that reflection and remorse are where the business of Learning takes place in a meaningful way and is the time for judgment to be determined. The distractions of life on the physical plane prevent all but the most rudimentary spiritual Learning there. Once you are free of those distractions and are in Spirit form and in direct consultation with your Guides, who are more advanced than you on their journeys, an honest, complete, and judicious view of your performance is undertaken in excruciating detail.

Imagine an enormous scale, the kind with a basket on each side of a balance beam, and imagine as all your good thoughts, words, and deeds are placed in one basket and all your bad thoughts, words, and deeds are placed in the other. Of course, the Divine already knows what the tally will be, but it is necessary for you to know too, and to reflect on all the things going into the baskets, one thought, word, and deed at a time. "Yes, you did that. Yes, you could have done it differently. Yes, you would have been better off and so would those around you have been better off had you done that differently. Yes, you feel deep remorse for what you did in that instance. Yes, you apologize to all those who were adversely affected. Yes, you promise not to do it again. Yes, you are proud of the way you behaved there. That was helpful for all concerned. You are pleased with that and will continue to behave in that manner." And so on. This process continues for every thought you had, every word you spoke, and every action you took, both good and bad, throughout your entire incarnation.

> *Narrator: I remember getting a message, through a medium, from the general I was wounded with in Vietnam. This message came during a medium session that is part of the service in a Spiritualist Church. The medium knew nothing of this general, and I had not known he had passed into Spirit nor even thought about him in years. The general was sorry he got us all wounded because it was at his discretion that we landed at that South Vietnamese artillery firebase. We tried to visit earlier in the day but saw the base take incoming fire while we were circling to land. The general decided we would try again after lunch. We were dropped off quickly, and the helicopter departed. When the helicopter came back and landed to pick us up, we received mortar fire. Some South Vietnamese army soldiers were killed, and all three Americans in our landing party, including the general and me, were wounded. The North Vietnamese*

army unit lobbing mortar shells that morning would know that somebody important would be visiting in a US Army helicopter so late in the war, so we gave them a wonderful target of opportunity. Of course, it was only because the general wanted to go there that we went at all. The helicopter took only some slight damage from mortar fragments, and we were able to get on board and fly directly to the hospital in Saigon to get patched up. The general's apology this many years later was easy to accept, however unexpected, because I never really blamed him for what happened. It was a war, after all, and people on both sides were constantly trying to kill each other. But it was clearly important for the general to make this apology, and I understand that this is an essential element of all post-life reviews. The general was working through the sorrow he felt for the consequences of his decision to visit that firebase, and I feel certain that he reached out to all the spirits of those who died and the others who were wounded, on both sides, not just to me.

Judgment

"Regardless of your chosen faith, at the end of your life's journey, your heart will

be measured in two ways. One, the weight of your conscience must far outweigh the weight of a feather. Two, any impurities in your heart must weigh no more than one feather. The purer your heart, the lighter your spirit will be. The lighter your spirit, the closer to light it will float. The closer to light it is permitted to go, the higher it will float. The higher it floats, the closer to God you will be. Your goal is to make your heart as light as a feather. The heavier the heart, the more chained to this hell it will remain."

Suzy Kassem

Mediums are earthly facilitators for souls to take responsibility for their thoughts, words, and deeds while on the Earth Plane. This is part of the process of apology and atonement.

When your physical body experiences death, your "spiritual dashboard" stops collecting information from that life and the cosmic "save" button is pressed, so to speak. Everything connected with you is in a celestial "file folder" with your name on it. How many brain cells were created or died during your lifetime? How many times did you have a positive or negative thought? What was the impact of each of your thoughts, words, and deeds as they rippled outward from you through others and indeed the Universe? What was the percentage of the good versus bad choices in this life? While those answers are known to the Divine and to your Guides, you will meet with your Guides and review the choices you made and their effects on yourself and others so you will come to understand the effects of all you did in this life on Earth. It is also when you learn how much progress, if any, your soul made toward Enlightenment and then Perfection. That review helps your Guides determine the next best step on your journey. To keep moving forward in your path of Learning, what will your Guides suggest for your next incarnation? Will they suggest you be human again or animal or something else entirely? Will you be male or female? Will you be white or a person of color? What country will you be born in and what will your social and economic situation be at birth? Will you be healthy or sickly? All these decisions are made based on the assessment of where you are, that is, how far you have progressed, in your individual spiritual journeys.

At the end of the life-review process, judgment is straightforward and based on the answers to these questions, among many others:

- Which side of the scale for this life is the heaviest—Love or Hate?
- What were the motivations for the Hate that was demonstrated?

- What were the motivations for avoiding Hate when Love won the argument?
- What happened as a result of the Hate that was demonstrated, and who or what suffered as a result?
- Which Hate motives need to be worked on in the next life?
- What sort of life provides the best opportunity to Learn the necessary lessons in the next incarnation?

Consequences

> *"Spiritual ownership begins when we take responsibility for our development and then begin walking on the path that leads to wisdom. We learn through our own mistakes. There is no doubt that the natural laws of the universe exist and affect everything that ever was or will be. Through following them, we choose the path of personal spiritual development where transformation and transcendence is possible."*
>
> *Rev. Dr. Eleanor Ruth Fisher*

The consequences for actions that do not advance The Divine Plan are simple. Your soul does not advance in its slow march to Enlightenment, Perfection, and eventual Reunion with The Divine One. Negative, Hate-based thoughts, words, and deeds earn you a place back on the Earth plane where conditions will be arranged that provide opportunities to behave better. This is like being held back a grade in school, and it slows down not only your individual progress toward Enlightenment, Perfection, and Reunification, but it also slows down the entire process of Reunification for the Universe. Any other consequences ascribed to this process are human constructs.

Punishment
Humans need to believe in punishment, and salvation, because they are fundamental to human nature as risk and reward markers that act as negative and positive incentives for moderating your behavior. And there is nothing wrong with that. "If you do that, you will rot in Hell" is a common warning you get from the pulpit and your parents and your friends and society in general. "If you are good to poor people, there is a place in Heaven for you" is another common theme. Many people believe in these concepts without reservation, but the truth is they are manifestations of your fears and desires, not fact.

When The Divine One gave you the gift of independent action, or Free Will, it came with no instructions or restrictions. You can and do choose any course of action you like as you go about your life. Some of the things you decide to think, say, or do are not helpful to you, your family, your friends, or others. Sure, you have Free Will and can do anything you want, but you most often know better than to do harmful things. Most healthy people know the Golden Rule and know right from wrong and know when they do wrong. You usually know if your bad behavior causes harm to yourself or others. It is these wrongs, these bad choices, that you must deal with, in consultation with your Guides, once you pass into spirit. This is a necessary part of the process of moving on, either forward or backward.

Once you clearly see and understand the thoughts, words, and deeds of your life that were "bad"—those that did not follow the goal of abandoning Hate in favor of Love—some punishment is necessary and appropriate. Punishment comes in many forms while on the Earth plane, but when you pass into Spirit, punishment is what you choose yourself, based on what you consider appropriate for each conscious, Hate-based thought, word, and deed. Think of the worst, scariest thing you can dream up. If that's how you want to punish yourself, then you will—and for however long you think is appropriate to impress upon yourself at the soul level to do everything possible to prevent your next human partner from doing it. Then you move on to the next thought, word, or deed you want to punish yourself for and determine the form of the punishment for that, too. Remember, none of this punishment is determined by anyone other than your own soul.

Because your Free Will is constant, you can also choose to ignore the Hateful things you did or still don't consider wrong, even after the life-review process. If you do that, you will simply find yourself in the same position, in a different life, where you will have another opportunity to do the right thing—the Love-based thing—and Learn from it. This can be repetitious if you do Hateful actions again and again until you finally "get it," change for the better, and move onward and upward.

For example, if you were cruel to animals, you could come back as the owner of a dog kennel and have the opportunity to demonstrate that you are committed to the Loving side of your nature and treat animals humanely. Or you could be born into a litter of pups owned by a pet abuser. The one inescapable consequence of bad behavior is that it will always catch up to you, either on the Earth plane or on the spirit planes, or both.

17

WHAT COMES NEXT

> *"I died as a mineral and became a plant, I died as a plant and rose to animal, I died as an animal and I was Man. Why should I fear? When was I less by dying?"*
>
> *Rumi*

Every soul's mission is to proceed as best it can toward Enlightenment and Perfection and eventual Reunification with the Divine.

The evaluation in "Heaven," as just described, determines the next best step in the evolution of each soul on its journey. That next step can be to return to some sort of physical life or remain on the spirit planes doing other tasks. Whatever comes next in the journey of your soul, you must shoulder your responsibility to help fulfill our Creator's Divine Plan: Reunification. So when your soul is ready and you are given no other task, then you are "reassigned" to a life on Earth or somewhere else on the physical plane. Earth is not the only planet on the physical plane that supports life. Souls have many other suitable locations to Learn while pursuing life in physical form.

The process of returning to life on the physical plane is what you call reincarnation. If you are to be reincarnated in a human, you choose the type of human in concert with your Spirit Guides. The family you are born into and the gender you are born with, as well as the country of birth and the social standing of the family, will be chosen to provide the opportunities best suited to the Learning assignment you are given. Then the chaos of life takes over, and you are pretty much on our own once again. You are never completely alone in your journey because a vast army of Guides will provide assistance if necessary and appropriate.

The path described in this narrative is long and not linear. Backsliding is common until souls Learn enough through the experiences in their journeys that they begin to exert more influence on themselves and their hosts and begin to gentle both of their conditions. In so doing they also help gentle the condition of the Universe and move it that much closer to Reunification.

ABOUT THE AUTHOR

Dennis Patrick Treece spent thirty years in the army. He saw combat and was wounded in action. After retiring from military life, Treece created a second career in security.

Treece is now retired and enjoys spending time with his wife, helping her with her art business, and working in the couple's vegetable garden.

SECTION SEVEN

Epilogue, Glossary

EPILOGUE

"Isn't it nice to think that tomorrow is a new day with no mistakes in it yet?"

L. M. Montgomery

"We have to allow ourselves to be loved by the people who really love us, the people who really matter. Too much of the time, we are blinded by our own pursuits of people to love us, people that don't even matter. It's time to put an end to this. It's time for us to let ourselves be loved."

C. JoyBell C.

One of the most spiritual things you can do is embrace your humanity. Connect with those around you today. Say, "I love

> *you," "I'm sorry," "I appreciate you," "I'm proud of you"…whatever you're feeling. Send random texts, write a cute note, embrace your truth, and share it…Cause a smile today for someone else…and give plenty of hugs.*
>
> ***Steve Maraboli***

What follows is the most important part of this narrative. Everything preceding it was provided only so this part might be understood more clearly.

Here's the thing. Humanity is (and has been for a long time) at a tipping point. You can see this as a challenge and an opportunity, or you can see it as a danger and a threat. If you rise to the challenge and do the right thing, then you can collectively proceed as usual on your path to Enlightenment, Perfection, and Reunification. If not, then you open the door to significant changes in the way things go for you on the Physical Plane.

Higher spirits are politely requesting that humanity change its behavior in certain ways that benefit humanity and the rest of Creation. These changes are listed below and apply to both humans and soul partners, acknowledging that each has a different way to address these things.

1. Think more Loving thoughts.
2. Say more Loving words.

3. Do more Loving things.
4. Tone down the Hate and the anger that comes with Hate. Don't sweat the small stuff and think: how will getting angry make this situation any better, make me any better, make others any better? (Remember that your anger has a ripple effect throughout all of Creation and will catch up to you.)
5. Remember your role in the Divine Plan: fulfill your obligation to embrace your journey toward Enlightenment and Perfection, which enables Reunification.

Are those requests unrealistic? For starters, they aren't requests; they're demands. If there is no other takeaway message, understand this: ***there is a God, your Creator, who has provided the Universe (and you) with some simple rules, and He is expecting them to eventually be followed in a conscious, competent manner, as evidenced by the choices you make.*** So far, for all the good things humans do, the scale is still tipped toward the side of Hate and not Love. Humanity is failing the test it has been given and shows no evidence that it will ever get it right. This is the problem. Failing tests by making wrong choices is part of the Plan, but with this proviso: *there has to be some indication that you all will eventually stop making so many bad choices and show signs that Humanity is on the path to redemption.* This is not happening.

Narrator: I am a great case in point, which is perhaps why I have been tasked with getting this message out to you. I get angry at little things. For example, if a shoe lace comes untied while I am walking, it makes me so angry. Intellectually, I think this is a silly little irritation, but I do not respond to it intellectually; I respond viscerally. If I shank a golf shot, which fortunately these days is rare, I go through a brief but intense and almost violent bout of anger—anger at myself, and no one else. My wife plays golf with me, and she feels the anger. It throws off her game. Such is the force of this brief wave of anger exploding out of me. I now know about thought energy and thought creation, and I know that this wave of anger is broadcast everywhere, not just in my mind and body, but also to my wife and the rest of Creation. If you multiply the power of one person's angry thought by the seven billion or so living humans on Earth, you begin to see the problem humanity causes the rest of Creation. We are, indeed "bothering the neighbors." Can I learn to moderate my thoughts and behavior? I certainly see the need for it, and I must dedicate the rest of my life on this Plane to doing just that. I am also hopeful that you will try to do the same.

For those who think humanity is too important to be punished, think again. Humankind is not so valuable in the Grand Plan that you are indispensable. True, humans are the best of the available training aids in all of Creation, but they are a stubborn, troublesome lot and not irreplaceable, and their lives are not sacred. If humans are wiped out, something will evolve to take their place. Maybe this next species will not cause so much trouble as it pursues Enlightenment and Perfection.

Remember this key point: *your soul and other soul-helpers and the Super-Souls that are working the case of humanity are all closely engaged in this effort but are not confident that humans can ever "get it" because of how they have evolved. They are past due to show signs of improvement. Because of this, you are being "politely requested" to moderate your Hate-based thoughts, words, and actions.*

This short narrative is a hard-copy reminder of that request. If you are to avoid another "course correction," you need to heed this call for action and get with the Divine Program. Listen to the angel on your right shoulder more than the devil on your left. If you don't heed this call, unlimited remedies are available to deal with troublesome humanity. For example, humans have the capability to cause their own extinction, so they should think about that and worry about that. An asteroid collision can achieve the same result. The dinosaurs were lost to something of the sort, and who wants that? Another approach is to provide humanity with a senior Super-Soul, or two, or three, like Jesus Christ was, to help people understand where they are and how to best move forward toward Enlightenment and Perfection. Wouldn't that be interesting? *So take a chill pill, get a grip, move toward The Light, and work on less Hate and more Love in your life.* The ball is now in your court.

End of Message.

GLOSSARY

"If you tell the Marines to secure a building, they will put riflemen around it and surround it with barbed wire. If you tell the Air Force to secure a building, they will lease it or buy it. If you tell the Navy to secure a building, they will empty it and close it down. And if you tell the Army to secure a building, they will lock the doors."

Sign in the Riyadh Headquarters of US Central Command during Desert Shield and Desert Storm

Narrator: Sometimes words you think you know well have much different meanings when used by someone else. The quotation above served as a reminder of this fact where all the armed services were working together to win a war and needed to communicate clearly; but often didn't, and were never sure why…until they were shown the sign. So what follows are some otherwise commonly used terms that have different interpretations, and it's important to know the Guide's definitions here so its message is properly delivered and understood. I am providing you the definitions for these terms as they were explained to me.

- "Creation" and the "Universe" and the "Cosmos" are the same thing for this narrative and are used interchangeably throughout.
- "Hate" is a loaded word with many human interpretations and shades of meaning. In the context of this narrative Hate is a term used to describe any and all negative thoughts, words, and deeds. Hate can be accurately described as "the dark side" of just about any emotion. Anger, for example, is a common manifestation of Hate. The problem with Hate is that hatred and all hateful thoughts act like a drag chute on the process of Reunification.
- "Heaven" is a common enough concept among most human faiths. Know that what you will recognize as heaven does exist, but it bears little resemblance to what most humans think it is like.

- "Hell" is also a common concept among most human faiths, but it does not exist except in human thoughts. Throughout human history, the fear of "going to hell" has been a powerful deterrent against vile actions, or even minor transgressions, but however useful the concept is, it is a human construct and nothing more. What actually passes for what humans think of as "hell" is discussed in chapter 15.
- "Learning" also has a different, fundamental meaning in this narrative than most humans would give it. It is not what you are used to thinking of as learning, like learning to ride a bicycle, learning a foreign language, or learning how to play poker. The process by which you Learn (with a capital "L") is by making mistakes. In so doing, you will suffer in countless ways, both physical and emotional. You will also cause others to suffer, both physically and emotionally. When you, as a single soul on your spiritual journey, come to realize that there is more to life than just going through it, and that Hate is unnecessary and Love is necessary, then you are starting on the path toward Enlightenment.
- "Love" as used here is not romantic love or paternal love or love of country, or anything of that nature. It is more like a deep respect and understanding at the soul level. Love with a

capital "L" is a fundamental force throughout Creation and has no qualifiers. There is simply no way to be partially loving here, no such thing as loving halfway. This is an all-the-way-or-nothing proposition. Example: someone brutally murders your children. You must Love them. You do not have to love what they did or who they are in this human incarnation, but you must recognize that they are, like you, a flawed human with an immortal soul doing its best (or not) to keep the human under control. That is the soul's task, and both the human and the soul are to be Loved. The human who murdered your children will be punished, most likely on Earth and definitely after passing into Spirit, and you may revel in their punishment, all the while Loving them. This is hard to comprehend in your world, but you must try because it is your Divine mission to do so.

- "Religion" also needs clarification. While this narrative is religious, it is not about religion. The story that unfolds in this narrative about The Divine One and the Meaning of Life, among other revelations, is not meant to threaten any religion or belief system. All readers are free to decide for themselves if what is contained here is something they can accept. Try to keep an open mind, and try not to get defensive over any divergence from what you have been told to believe or what you have come to believe on your own. It is hoped that you can find a way to integrate this into your current faith without overreacting to what may seem to you to be complete heresy and fantasy. Clearly, if there were one "true" religion, everyone would be practicing it. Just like if there were one perfect automobile, you would all be driving it. However, you can look in any parking lot to see the evidence of two things that clarify this point: "free will" and lack of certainty. You are free to choose any car you can afford, and nobody is certain there is a perfect car, so you buy what best meets your wants or needs. People are famous for divergent opinions on everything, including religion, so they practice different religions or no religion at all. Who is right? Actually, religions in the sense that you know them are artificial constructs of humans and need to be seen in that light. But if it gives you comfort to go to a house of worship, then by all means go. Just remember that the Divine One did not give any of them to you. Rather, He gave them all to you when he gave you Free Will, but this did not come with any endorsements.

- "Souls" are nonphysical spirits and are conscious fragments of The Divine One Himself. Simple-Souls are individual fragments on their spiritual journeys. Compound-Souls are multiple souls who have joined together as described in the chapter on Souls. Super-Souls are very advanced conglomerations of Compound-Souls who have achieved Perfection. Conglomerations of souls can be referred to as "Pods," and they are of many different magnitudes. That is, each Pod will consist of some number of souls at the same level of development, but there is no set number. The basic thing to know about souls is that the larger the Pod, the more Divine Energy the soul has, and with this comes Divine Power, Divine Authority, and Divine Responsibility.

- "Spirit Guides" are Compound-Souls or Super-Souls of various magnitudes who are assigned to watch over one or more Simple-Souls or lesser Compound-Souls and their physical partners, including humans. They provide guidance and assistance and some intervention and of course can call on even more powerful intervention from larger Pods of Super-Souls if needed. They are with all of you constantly. When you sleep and dream, they are in much more direct contact with you than when you are awake. You often refer to your Guides as "guardian angels," and that is an accurate way to think of them.

- "Spiritual Journeys" consist of a soul-quest having three objectives. The first objective is to realize that there is more to existence than your own soul and your life with a physical partner and that doing good things is better than doing bad things. Understanding and totally living the Golden Rule is a good initial start for Enlightenment, the first objective. The second major objective is the attainment of Perfection, which is the fundamental realization that Hate is completely unnecessary and is completely abandoned while Love is seen as completely necessary and is adopted totally as the fundamental framework for your every thought, word, and deed. The final objective is the complete loss of individual or group identity and merger with the Divine One Himself—when The Divine judges you are ready. When all souls have achieved this state, then Divine Reunification is achieved.

- "The Devil" exists, but only inasmuch as you have created him. In other words, there is no devil except in your mind. You need someone to blame when things go badly, when you go badly, so you have created the ultimate fall guy. Who better than an angel cast out of heaven? Humanity fears anything that affects its survival, so loss of control, uncertainty, mistakes, and bad behavior can lead to problems you would rather not take the rap for, so you have conveniently created an entity that can be blamed for pretty much anything negative. But deep down,

you know that this devil you fear is actually the part of you that can, and does, think bad thoughts, say bad words, and do bad things.
- "Thought" is a word you think you know well, but in the context of this narrative, "thought" is a powerful manifestation of mental energy that can be felt throughout the Universe. Human thoughts, more than thoughts from any other physical being, are like the neighbor's stereo speakers turned to full volume at 2 a.m. on a workday. This was not planned; it was simply the way the human being developed. Your brain is rooted in the physical plane, but your mind creates thoughts on a higher vibration than you are. As a consequence, your thoughts can be annoying on the energy planes when they stray from Loving to anger and Hating. Since thought creation is a given on the energy planes, you should understand how important it is for humanity to "turn down the volume" by thinking more positive, Loving, thoughts.
- "Time." Most people think they are temporal beings living in a linear fashion from birth to death. This is true for humans but not *souls*. Your soul is not temporal or linear. You simply find yourself conscious right now in a time-linear place, in human form, where you have no conscious frame of reference to the nonlinear timelessness of your Spirit-self. For humanity,